I0790568

EVERY WOMAN IS A FEMALE *BUT NOT* EVERY FEMALE IS A WOMAN

The Process Leads to Discovery

Minister Roberta L Robertson

authorHOUSE

AuthorHouse™
1663 Liberty Drive
Bloomington, IN 47403
www.authorhouse.com
Phone: 833-262-8899

Published by AuthorHouse 06/09/2022

ISBN: 978-1-6655-6164-8 (sc)
ISBN: 978-1-6655-6163-1 (hc)
ISBN: 978-1-6655-6165-5 (e)

Library of Congress Control Number: 2022910900

Print information available on the last page.

The Auther's Prayer for the Reader

Girlfriend, as you engulf yourself into these pages and submit to this journey of the transition from female to Godly Womanhood, I have already prayed that God will surround you with His presence. I pray for restoration, deliverance, and transformation by renewing your mind and spirit. And you receive salvation, and His abundance and love will guide you to your divine purpose and calling.

Dear Abba,

You are divine in every way, and there is no other like You. I am thankful You have drawn these individual spirits to this book for new elevation levels and dimensions.

I pray Your Holy Spirit falls upon them, and the breath of life exhaled into them, and You will allow no weapon formed against them to prosper.

I declare You increase their capacity, and they are filled with hope and given peace as they enter into this healing season without limitations.

I bind and cancel every enemy's assignment to distract them from receiving what this book intended—a life of abundance, renewal, revelation, and transformation into the new.

I decree that Your power and spirit will fall upon them, and they are liberated from their bruises and brokenness. And they see clearly through Your lens Lord and lean not on their own understanding.

Let their hearts rest upon You, Father, for supernatural healing and restoration and deliverance.

In the mighty name of Jesus Christ, our Lord and Savior, Amen

CONTENTS

DEDICATION

I want to dedicate this book to every female with a desire to reach a place of wholeness, which is intentional about the transition and discovery to full Godly Womanhood and is not afraid of the testimony God has placed inside of them. Every female struggling with defining themselves by worldly depictions such as sex, temptations, marriage, friendships, past wounds, jobs, position, giving birth, material status, or physical beauty. And to every female who might be operating in their female state versus their mature woman state of mind.

I misunderstood so much about the transition and the process of grasping Godly Womanhood; I completely crashed and burned because I allowed the world to define my worth and my value rather than God, who created me. The further away I got from God, the closer I was to sin, and the closer I was to God, the further away I was from sin. I endured many trials and self-afflictions, but God spoke to me when I was completely resistant. He provided a place of refuge, and while doing so, He says because His grace sustained me through much opposition, many struggles, and dark valleys, I would be his mouthpiece to many women who would fight with this same transition.

I had no idea what that meant nor why He would choose me for this assignment. However, I was not immediately obedient to His plan and purpose to thrust me into this very moment. I later discovered that my condition would affirm God's position for me. God knew that it would be at this appointed time I would share with you everything that I had come through, everything that I had survived, everything that I had outlasted, and everything that I outlived. Everything that I pressed through and every tear I shed was God transitioning me from female to Godly Womanhood, so I could share my testimony and pour into you.

I pray that God will do just as he promised through the upcoming pages of this book. I intend to meet you right where you are in your season of transition. It doesn't matter if you are going through difficult times, in an identity crisis, are in a pit of fire, in the middle of a red sea, or are lost in the wilderness; God wants to solicit your participation so you can be made whole.

In your darkest valley, you can find refuge. If you are up against your goliath, He will give you extraordinary strength even if you are unclear of your purpose or torn up from the floor up. God is not intimidated by the size of your problem. Instead, God is using my voice to help prepare and shift you from female to Godly Womanhood so that you can discover the purpose of what God has declared over your life.

FOREWORD

This book that you now hold in your hand is the beginning of a beautiful journey that will expose the uncomfortable places and spaces preventing you from becoming whole. If you know what it feels like to be unloved, if you experienced emotional disconnection, if a little girl is hiding behind the mask of social media "likes" and "followers," if you are running from past mistakes, if you are in a painful and damaging relationship, if you are coming out of a traumatic past, if you've had your share of broken and empty promises, or whether you've successfully accomplished your goals come take this walk with Minister "Ro."

After the death of Moses, Joshua was given the task of leading the next generation to the 'Promised Land.' God tells Joshua, "This is my command – be strong and courageous! Do not be afraid or discouraged. For the LORD your God is with you wherever you go." Joshua 1:9 (NLT). Get comfortable being uncomfortable at times. Watch the maturation process unfold through each chapter: joy, pain, anger, peace, fear, courage, hope, despair, and a range of other emotions will be released once you begin the required work of investing honestly in yourself.

You will hear the call to become lovestruck with yourself through the evolution of becoming a woman... the woman God intended you to be. There is no doubt that whether you are a young adult or in your latter season, you will glean from the transparency and honesty contained within the pages. Embrace the authenticity of Minister Ro's' gift to express the road she traveled from "Female to a Woman!" There will be an awakening fanned and fueled by the articulated message as you progress from one chapter to the next.

Your presence is requested! Do the work. Cry the tears. Turn the page. Answer the questions. Process your feelings. Take the notes. Your highlighter will be busy. Your Breakthrough is on the horizon. Your Gift is awaiting. Your Future is calling. The Sacrifice is worth it.

This could easily be a theologically driven version of "How Stella got her groove back." The *difference* is throughout the process, you will begin to recognize whose you are in Christ and His purpose for your life. The *difference* is you will begin to forgive yourself and transition into the WOMAN GOD DESIGNED YOU to be. The *difference* is you will now dismantle the mind of a female and begin the evolution into Womanhood. The *difference* is that you will be encouraged, comforted, refreshed, healed, and transformed within the pages of this book. Welcome to Womanhood.

Pastor Michael J. Henderson

INTRODUCTION

The Transformation to Godly Womanhood

Hello Girlfriend, can we talk some real talk? The bible says that before you were in your mother's womb, God knew what your biological makeup would be. And based on your spiritual and physical makeup, there was an assignment and anointing prophesied over your life. The truth of the matter is, "For we are God's masterpiece. He has created us anew in Christ Jesus, so we can do the good things he planned for us long ago." (Ephesians 2:10, NLT). He knew the creation of every woman would demonstrate purpose, and they would become pioneers and forerunners all over the earth. However, God did not lay out the detailed step-by-step process of becoming that Proverbs 31(P-31) woman. Even though He knows the beginning and the end, there is no complete picture of our path. Unfortunately, God doesn't conduct business that way. If He were to provide us with the full view, there would be no need for a test, no reason to hope, have faith, or rely on Him.

You are born female, but life experiences will transform you from female to *Godly Womanhood*. There is evidence of fruit in the transformation, but knowing which tree to eat from will determine how fruitful you will become. A female is guided to the wrong tree, which causes her to be disobedient and lean on her own understanding. Her emotions and her flesh easily persuade her. It causes postponement in her purpose and causes conflicts with her anointed purpose and identity. It does not mean the transformation will not occur, but while she is leaning, God will have to prop her back up in the correct position, provide her with nutrients and water, and give her plenty of sunshine.

When God steps in to reposition you, He must remove all the dead leaves, cut off all the branches, and fertilize you. Jesus said, "I am the true vine, and my Father is the gardener. "He cuts off every branch in me that bears no fruit, while every branch that does bear fruit, he prunes so that it will be even more fruitful" (John 15:1-2, NIV).

A transformation into *Godly Womanhood* will be an evolving moment. This process will not come without some pain and labor. But, it will be a crucial outcome of you giving birth to understanding why *Every Woman is a Female but not Every Female is a Woman.*

Thanks to Eve, the female gender will endure the push and pull from female to *Godly Womanhood* until the day they die. And I don't say this in a disparaging or hateful way. We

When God steps in to reposition you, He must remove all the dead leaves, cut off all the branches, and fertilize you.

all have a little bit of Eve in us and have been in the same boat, or we would not be seeking to get to the transition point. But, then, as long as God has placed an anointing and purpose in you, the enemy will come after you. He will invade your life to minimize, nullify, and attempt to destroy your potential.

So, where did this push and pull begin? Well, I'm glad you asked. We can certainly start in the book of Genesis, where the creation of woman began. Undoubtedly, God already knew the outcome in the garden that Eve would fall for the enemy's craftiness and cunningness. In Genesis 3:15-16 KJV, God gave the consequences of Eve's action, which would prevail over humanity and all generations of the female gender.

Let's break this down from my perspective; in my interpretation, the slithering snake did not approach Adam; he went directly to Eve. Thus, we can assume the actions of the serpent is intentional. His goal was to persuade Eve to believe and do something other than what God directed her. He wanted to create doubt in her mind. Why do you think this occurred? Because the enemy knew Eve was the most vulnerable. He knew he could seduce her to feel more than what God purposed her for in the garden, using this moment to cause disruption and discourse between the Kingdom of God and the kingdom of the devil. The enemy knew the anointing that God placed on the inside of women. I believe this is where opposition began between how we would struggle with the push and pull from female to *Godly Womanhood*.

Well, nothing has changed today; the enemy is still diligently on an assignment in pursuit to distract every woman from following God's command, from receiving what God has promised, and from a life of abundance and favor. The devil was right there and was a receiver of God's consequences for both him and Eve. Knowing there would be enmity between him and the woman, the enemy would be in full pursuit. So, he set out on his assignment to strategically target women, create discourse, insecurities, mental confusion, identity struggle, fear, pain, rejection, trauma, abuse, lack of self-worth, shame for mistakes, anger, and hatred towards each other. The caveat to Genesis 3:15-16 KJV is found in the latter part of verse 16 when God lays out Satan's ultimate destruction of his death, which through the woman's seed, Christ Jesus came taking away his sting, which is sin.

The enemy is ambitious and intentional about taking you out. He will target your mind creating warfare with the powers of principalities. The struggle is real! Make no mistake about it; just like he persuaded Eve to eat the forbidden fruit, he will try to convince you of where you stand with God. Satan is a destructive mechanism and wants to kill you, destroy you, and snatch out the potential God placed inside you. However, the one thing about God is that He takes no mess from Satan. God will unclog and uncap everything the enemy closes off because He knows the plans, He has for you (Jeremiah 29:11, NIV). Therefore, your femininity is not solely attached to the enemy's pursuit of you through God's creation. But there is a transition from female to *Godly*

Womanhood, and it's not without attacks from the enemy and seasons of struggle. The enemy will use every fragile thing in your spirit against you during his continuous pursuit to attempt destruction. But listen, God promises us strength in the time of weariness. (Isaiah 40:29, NIV)

Suppose you are in the midst of an attack from the enemy. Or have you taken a bite of forbidden fruit and gone through overwhelming experiences in your life, or perhaps you're amid temptation. You are being tested to overcome inadequacies at this very moment. Whatever your opposition, God may be allowing this push and pull situation to transition you from female to *Godly Womanhood* and draw you nearer to Him. Look at it this way; whatever crisis you face, it can be an opportunity. The crisis will cause you to seek Him and, in turn, cause you to change your life or circumstances. So how do you fight back? First, although we are called to speak to the devil, we are never to have discussions with him. Second, you must put on the whole armor of God and allow Him to prepare you for the battle against the schemes of the devil (Ephesians 6:10, ESV). And last, trust God's process! For Him to make his work complete in you, you must push when the pain is the greatest to give birth to your potential and discovery.

Are you ready to start the process from female to *Godly Womanhood?* If so, turn the page and let me share with you the process and testimony of how God used my seasons of struggles and self-dependency and turned them into a relationship of trusting Him and transforming me from female to *Godly Womanhood?*

CHAPTER ONE

THE PROCESS

"Everything God allows to come our way is always with purpose. He uses even the greatest errors and deepest pains to mold us into a better person."

Kingsley Glass

Hello, mic check, testing one, two, and three! Can you hear me, girlfriend! I just wanted to make sure you could hear the sound of my voice. Because what's coming up next is the sound of integrity, transparency, and downright rawness in the following few pages. The process from female to a woman is not something we catapult over a bridge and arrive at. It will not be a microwavable process.

There is no magic potion or quick remedy for transitioning from female into *Godly Womanhood.*

And, if you believe it's as easy as that, you may be operating with a female state of mind and are in definite need of plunging into understanding this process.

So, naturally, there may be a belief and the assumption that there is a correlation between femininity and womanhood. There may even be an assumption our femininity connects us to our purpose. Well, that may be partially true, but there is more to this hypothesis. So, if you explore with me, we might find a more comprehensive way to examine this ideology.

What is a *process?* Collins English dictionary says a process is a series of actions carried out to achieve a particular result. So, the word process is an action word that requires something to happen or occur to reach an outcome. The King James dictionary defines process as a proceeding or moving forward; progressive course; tendency; as the process of man's desire.

The transition from female to *Godly Womanhood* requires shaking off the old and stepping into the new. So, there is a "New You" inside of you that God is looking to process. He's had His eye on us and designed us for glorious living; part of the overall purpose He is working out in everything and each of us. (Ephesians 1:12, MSG)

Occasionally God will initiate your participation in the process. And it will require a breakdown and dismantling of the "Old You" and deep cleaning from the inner core out. Other times God will take His hands off you, and He will allow your situation or circumstances to remold you for His good. The promises of God are a process. He will provide you with His promises, but you will have to take some trips through the desert. And understand there is no expiration date on the promises of God. He is waiting on your participation. He wants to make you the head and not the tail. (Deuteronomy 28:13, NIV)

I describe the "Old You" as the broken part of us constructed just by living, poor choices, and all the woundedness that comes with it. This female is shaped through a process of deep hurt, scars, deficient identity, and self-appointed actions. But, on the other hand, the "New You "is authentic and transformed because the "Old You" helps discover who you are in Christ Jesus.

Is it a probability that you have been approaching things backward? What if you step out of the box just for a moment and consider that first? God wants you to know who you are in Him rather than what you are purposed to do. So drop the mic on that one!

God will tap you on your proverbial shoulder and remind you; that He made you in His image (Genesis 1:26-27, KJV). Yes, God not only wants you to know who you are but whose you are! Until you identify and accept who He fashioned you to be, your purpose and potential will remain indistinct. I believe there is a connection between our identity and the transition from female to *Godly Womanhood*. And without a doubt, it will take some work to get through the process. In reality, we will probably spend our entire life in the process. However, the ultimate goal is to stay in the race, reach the transition point, and go beyond the crossroads.

Life has no postponements, and it hurled me right into the season and process from female to *Godly Womanhood.* I took to the mentality of identifying myself with worldly depictions, indulging and sipping on everything that would make my flesh feel good. Sound familiar? It was like sipping on a hot cup of coffee or tea daily; once I digested the things of this world, it was like producing caffeine adrenaline. The flesh can become so addicted to the world that our body will go through withdrawals when we attempt to disengage. My addiction was men because I was looking for love in all the wrong places, finding daddy, and filling the pain from my wounds. They became my coffee, sex became my tea, and I kept adding sugar until I could taste the sweetness of their flesh.

Just like the coffee or tea filling my body and creating that addiction, so did the spirit of those men. Every time I had a physical encounter with them, it filled my spirit with their spirit. If they were evil, my spirit encountered evil; if they were addicted to anything, my spirit would experience their addictions; if broken, my spirit would become attached to their brokenness. This coffee or tea filled my spirit with every type of sugar and creamer I could not even imagine. In other words, I bit the forbidden fruit! My internal spirit was already filled with unhealthy spirits; nonetheless, my cup was overrunning with these men's added ingredients. I was living a Burger King life; I had it my way! But, in reality, I was tore-up from the floor up!

Why? Because I thought as a female, and I made decisions as a female. Let's pause there for a moment, and let me show you how Satan works. All the wounds from my childhood, the molestation, rape, and emotional/physical abuse caused me to seek fulfillment in the most violated and broken areas in my life. The enemy intended to destroy me early and attempt to disrupt God's plans for me. Satan is a perpetual liar, and when he meets up with Eve in the garden, he lies to her. And once she ate of the forbidden fruit, he called her out on her nakedness, making her feel ashamed of her body and self-image. It's no different for us.

Because we don't like ourselves, we will do all kinds of dumb crap. Then, after we do all the dumb stuff, Satan will use it against us to make us feel worthless. His full intent was to create strongholds that would cause me to sin and lose sight of my potential and who God created me to be. However, the devil didn't know his setup was prepping me for my get-up!

Are you reading this and feeling an association or a disconnect with yourself? Well, girlfriend! I won't apologize for the transparency because this is what it will take for you to open up about your own truths and realities. And bring revelation about why *Every Woman is a Female and not Every Female is a Woman.* So, for example, your coffee might not have been as dark as mine, or maybe you didn't experience a coffee addiction at all. But, on the other hand, it may have been a Coke and Rum addiction, you get the point, right. So, the question is, when you took a bite of the forbidden fruit, did it cause you to feel ashamed of who you were? If so, you have to get to a place of hunger and thirst after righteousness (Matthew 5). You must dismiss the spirit of discouragement and defeat and look at every setback as a comeback.

Now, girlfriend, we can't blame the devil for everything. We have to have some accountability on our part. God does give us something called free will. It wasn't until I became exhausted from the perplexities of life, addiction of brokenness, playing the victim, shame, failed relationships, embarrassment, and reaching rock bottom that I decided I needed to seek healing and deliverance.

I'm not speaking about material possessions but a spiritual rock bottom. It was evident I became codependent in a cycle of dysfunction and was at a place where I expected God to be Houdini, jump at my request and change the very circumstances I shaped. The point is that I used what was feminine to gain what I was lacking or wanted, not what I needed, and it defined "who" I was not.

God could have turned off the cycle in my life at any time, but He allowed me to wallow in my mess. Thank God He did! Understanding the struggles in your life is part of your destiny process. Some of your most significant growth spurts are in and during the struggle. They are the prerequisite to your new destination. The more you resist the process of struggle, the longer you will remain in the battle.

The process of transformation was occurring, and I had no idea. Are you experiencing any cycles in your life, emotional shopping, uncontrolled anger, looking for love in all the wrong places, depression, or feeling broken or damaged? Well, get ready, girl! You are about to get your breakthrough. At the end of this chapter, I want you to jot down everything keeping you in bondage and preventing you from choosing to find revelation. (note 1) We will break the yokes of the enemy and take back the territory of your life.

God sees treasure and beauty in us because we are precious in His eyes (Isaiah 43:4, ESV). Therefore, everything you go through will be necessary, and wisdom will come through every experience and poor decision. God will interrupt your plan in His time. When your life is stinky like the dumping ground, God will still see you as a treasure. There is a meaning behind His glories, and God expects us to pursue them.

God will allow the wounds so that you can reach a point of "choice." A choice to start the process of revelation to who He created you to be. You can choose to pursue a covenant with Him and seek *Godly Womanhood* and step out of your self-driven motives, your addictions, your depression, your brokenness, a victim mindset, a deceiving spirit, or having it your way. The choice is yours!

You might be asking, what if you don't make a choice? Let's say the circumstances that God allows can dictate an outcome for you. When you wrestle with God, it will end up in two ways. First, He will stop wrestling with you for a while and then find someone else to wrestle with. Second, your blessing will prevail if you wrestle with God long enough.

One of the most amazing things about God is He knows when you're tired and broken, but you have to know when you are tired and broken. So, when He says rest your cares upon Him, He will sustain you because God is faithful to His word. However, being broken doesn't mean you give up. It just means you choose not to lean on your own understanding. But renew your mind, body, and soul, and allow your spirit to be transformed. It requires you to remove some things or people from your life, take time out, set priorities, be quiet, and listen to God's voice.

In some cases, you might even find you are pulled or yanked into the season God wants based on your circumstances. But, girlfriend, God will put His foot on the peddle and accelerate no matter what season you are in. He will show up when and how He chooses, even when you least expect it in your conversations or actions. No matter how comfortable or calculating your routine, not even your plans or hidden agendas will change His interruption. You can attempt to pivot to avoid Him, but it won't override His outcome. God will use your situation to gain revelation and draw out the godly woman in you. We look for everything to define us and make us whole except the God who created us. Therefore, we must stop looking for someone to save us from the anguish of wounds and our past. Let's explore this for a moment.

You may invest your entire life competing with people trying to prove you are somebody and still feel like a nobody. So, let me awaken the pink elephant in the room. Are you a married female who has identified herself with a marriage that defines who you are? If you have started your wedding hoping that it will help you be all you can be, turn around and "shut the front door" because it will not happen. The process from female to *Godly Womanhood* must start before marriage.

Bringing a female mentality into a marriage will cause a strain producing the marriage to be unequally yoked. And no real godly man desires a selfish female looking to satisfy their own needs. I'm just saying!

Maybe you have been shacking up for the last five years, and you're waiting for the dude to make that big proposal. The female in you says he loves me, and I need to be patient a little longer. But, unfortunately, why would he drink just one glass of milk when he is getting the whole cow for free. The godly woman would value her treasures and know her worth. The absence of a holy woman will always fill the presence of a worldly female!

Are you a female corporate leader leading an organization, a female pastor leading a congregation, or the agency's first female president? Regardless of your title or position, you can find yourselves leading, guiding, and operating with a female mindset. However, there is one thing that I know for sure; status does not entitle you to *Godly Womanhood*. You can be insecure and lack emotional intelligence, spiritual maturity, or even wear masks to cover who God created you.

You can have the wounded "little girl" syndrome and not be delivered from all the hurt and trauma of your childhood. Every decision you make is made by the wounded little girl and not the mature woman. Why would I entertain this? Well, let me make this portrait a bit more colorful for you! If you are in a female lead role, leading in any capacity, indulging messy work environments, dysfunctional relationships, communities, agencies, or churches, you haven't fully embraced *Godly Womanhood*. You are not leading with a kingdom mindset and are operating as a wounded leader. That's a whole different book right there!

A primary example is that you could find yourselves at an executive level at your employment and oversee another more intelligent woman. And your female reaction kicks in, and you become jealous and insecure instead of embracing her intellect and knowledge. That right there is identified as a female attitude!

Are you tired of allowing the devil to create havoc in your life? Are you tired of creating havoc in your life and other folks' life? Are you ready to stop filling your cup up with all that nasty sugar, then make a choice? Step in the process and allow God to work a strategized plan for your life.

The process requires a strategy that involves God, acceptance, intentional pursuit, deliverance, determination, and commitment. Unconsciously and consciously, as you explore life, you will experience environments, people, and circumstances dressed in camouflage and tempting you to take Satan's bait. Even your own choices become the catalyst for your development into *Godly Womanhood*, good or bad. However, establishing a godly strategy requires you to stop faking the funk, eliminate the imposter syndrome, blaming others for your poor choices, and get real with the false premises you have mirrored your identity.

The proper strategy starts with recognizing you are operating as a female and that your behavior, characteristics, and decisions exemplify the attributes of a female. If you are offended and you are at the point of tossing this book to the side, hold your horses. The reality is that no female is born with the maturity of full *Godly Womanhood*. It is exposure to life and His word that helps you develop.

Let me be 100 with you! A female is one of *birth,* but a woman is one of *exposure.* If you exemplify a female attitude, you will never be satisfied, you will be trapped in your flesh, never be content, and you will always be preoccupied with what you don't have. A female will spend more time complaining, never being thankful for the little things, being self-absorbed, and only praying in the darkness of a valley. The truth of the matter is that we have all been there, and if you can't admit it, I'm okay with you tossing this book for now. You're just not ready for the process!

---

*A Female is one of birth, but a woman
is a matter of exposure.*

You must allow God to be the governor over the strategy. Even in the season when you are consciously operating as a female, God is strategizing your outcome. He doesn't expect you to sit back and not get your hands dirty. God does require efforts on your part. In the Bible, the disciple, James, made it clear, "Faith without works is dead"(James 2:26, KJV). If you are not putting in the work, don't expect results, and the result is a life unchanged.

The process is subject to a commitment, and the responsibility of the obligation is subject to a fight. You can't be a wimp when it comes to the stones thrown at you. Like David, you'll need your slingshot to fight every giant coming against you in this process. Yes, you're going to enter into a dog fight, but you will win the battle because no weapon formed against you will succeed (Isaiah 54:17, NASB). How God shapes you connects you to who you are and is determined by your beliefs.

The process requires a new belief system. You must get rid of the old to focus on the new. You can't mix the old with the new and expect promising results. It's like putting fresh deodorant under a dirty armpit; it still stinks. There is no way for you to mix your female characteristics with a godly woman character and expect the process to lead to discovery. The method of new beliefs requires disengaging your faulty beliefs.

Faulty belief systems often plague us due to our upbringing, generational standards, and environments. A predisposition causes us to carry the old beliefs based on those environments and standards. It can cause us to contradict what we believe God has planned for us in our life. We sabotage ourselves or blessings because we don't think we deserve to be elevated or transitioned.

You must be intentional about your approach to the process and be open to transparency and transformation. Be honest with where you are. Are you spiritually out of shape? Are you not prepared to run this race? Are you torn up from the floor up? Admit it! Will you lose some fights? Absolutely! The race is not to the swift nor to the strong but to those who endure to the end. (Ecclesiastes 9:11, ESV)

"The race is not to the swift nor to the strong
but to those who endure to the end."
Ecclesiastes 9:11
English Standard Version

If you choose to start this process, know that you will find strength in God, and Holy Spirit is always with those who accept Him. His power will strongly influence you and help you overcome all obstacles in your process. He will watch over you, and He will always be your guiding light.

Are you still with me? Good, let's keep it pushing! So, get your gloves, workout gear, helmet, and baby oil; let's start this fight and process and win this battle.

NOTE 1

My Devotional Thoughts

Jot down everything keeping you in bondage and preventing you from choosing to find revelation.

Prayer

Gracious Father, I am broken and displaced. And I have been leaning on my own understanding of who I am. I want to be set free and made whole, and I asked You to break every stronghold over my life and walk with me through this process from female to Godly Womanhood. In Jesus' Name, Amen

Scriptures of Meditation

"For I am confident of this very thing, that He who began a good work in you will perfect it until the day of Christ Jesus." (Philippians 1:6, NASB)

"And let endurance have its perfect result so that you may be perfect and complete, lacking in nothing." (James 1:4, NASB)

"But the jar he was making did not turn out as he had hoped, so he crushed it into a lump of clay again and started over." (Jeremiah 18:4, NLT)

"I will put flesh and muscles on you and cover you with skin. I will put breath into you, and you will come to life. Then you will know that I am the LORD."
(Ezekiel 37:6, NLT)

"For you have need of endurance, so that when you have done the will of God, you may receive what is promised." (Hebrews 10:36, ESV)

"As for God, His way is blameless; The word of the Lord is tried; He is a shield to all who take refuge in Him." (Psalm 18:30, NASB)

"To everything, there is a season and a time to every purpose under the heaven." (Ecclesiastes 3:1, KJV)

"Let your roots grow down into him, and let your lives be built on him. Then your faith will grow strong in the truth you were taught, and you will overflow with thankfulness." (Colossians 2:7, NLT)

FEMALE VERSUS WOMAN

"Charm is deceptive, and beauty is fleeting;
But a woman who fears the LORD is to be praised."

Proverbs 31:30(NIV)

Girlfriend, before I get down to the grit of things, I want to start somewhat with a more formal approach. I want to invite you to the table for dinner. I have a special meal prepared for you in this chapter. I want to layout a 7-course meal, there will be a couple of side dishes, but I promise I will get to the meat of it all. I pray you are hungry and have an appetite for the transformation from female to *Godly Womanhood*. It may appear to be a bit monotonous while indulging in this chapter, but I assure you that if

18

you keep chewing, you'll be able to digest everything I've put on your plate.

If you expect any progress or application from this book, there must be a clear-cut understanding of the difference between females and a woman. As I bring clarity as to why *"Every Woman is a Female but not Every Female is a Woman,"* don't leave the table just yet. Instead, stay with me for a while and follow me as I break down the two ingredients.

The Societal definition of a female/woman

Let's break this down according to the *Nasdaq Board Diversity and Disclosure*. First, its new approved definition describes a female as an individual who self-identifies her gender as a woman, without regard to the individual's designated sex at birth. In other words, gender is not absolute in determining if you are female. Instead, gender is based on a personal sense of identity. Second, Nasdaq's definition implies that you can identify yourself as whatever you want as a female. You can identify yourself as a bird, but it doesn't make it accurate. You can identify yourself as a man, but it doesn't mean it is true.

Scientifically, a female's sex is determined at birth, establishing what God has already defined as a female. So when he pulled the rib from Adam to make Eve, it implies that God created Eve into a whole woman, but through the fall of man, He directed man to procreate.

And if the female is a result of procreation, then there is a process from female to woman. Now that was a lot to chew on, but I promise you will digest everything on this plate. Just keep chewing!

On the other hand, *Merriam Webster Dictionary* defines a female person as a woman or a girl, an individual of the sex typically capable of bearing young or producing eggs. What does this mean in laymen's terms? Webster is simply saying your sex determines if you are a female. However, there is some implication between the two definitions. Nasdaq implies women will use societal words to decide which category they will be placed in to define their gender. On the other hand, Webster says your birth solidifies your identity. So, it depends on which report you select and by who.

In my perspective, the fact that you are born female doesn't determine you to be a mature woman. For example, a female infant is a female but is not a woman. Also, an infant grows into a teenager and is a female, but she is still not a mature woman.

You cannot identify yourself as whatever you want because God created Eve and called her a woman. You probably stopped chewing right there! Drink some water and pause for a minute. Let's look at this thing more comprehensively. To sum this up, you can't change the fact that you are born female, but you can grow into the woman God created, purposed, and intended you to be. You must not focus on how things happen but on what God allowed to happen, which is your conception.

Please make no mistake about it; you were deliberately created! We are the masterpiece He created, and we don't get to alter His creation. I love the way Serita Jake so eloquently expresses it, "Being a Female is a matter of birth; being a woman is a matter of age, but being a lady is a matter of choice."

"Being a Female is a matter of birth; being a woman is a matter of age, but being a lady is a matter of choice."
Sarita Jakes

There is a forewarning here, and there are certain anomalies where females are born with male genitals called "Ambiguous genitalia," The external sex organs may not match the internal sex organs. Now I'm no expert in this area, but remember, the bible says, "God created all humanity in his image." (Genesis 1:27, KJV) Due to human sin and our girl Eve and Lucifer, we are deeply flawed, physically, morally, and emotionally jacked up. God intended for us to be blessed, but sin placed us under a curse, which is the source of every physical problem we face. And it does not exclude our moral and emotional issues. (Genesis 3:16-18, NIV)

Now that I've pleasured you with a full course meal and indulged you in a taste of this societal explanation of a female versus woman, I hope you are not full just yet. Let me prepare you for dessert, and let's move on to find out what God says about a female and a woman.

The biblical definition of a female/woman

The *King James dictionary* says, "A woman is a compound of womb and man; the female of the human race, grown to adult years. And the rib, which the Lord God had taken from the man, made her a woman" (Genesis 2). You are tasting this dessert and probably wondering what's in it. If you ask that question, I'm glad you asked because I will give you the ingredients in the following few paragraphs.

The word compound is two or more separate elements; thus, a womb gives birth to something, and God creates and sustains a man. You have here the element of the womb, and man, therefore, bringing forth a woman. Although God made a woman from a man, He identified two separate genders and roles for them. I believe God created a woman for a specific function not defined by societal terms but created her specifically for humanity. He made a woman for symmetry on the earth, and women are the final touch of His masterpiece of humankind. So, girlfriend, we are exceptional in every way!

The excellent model of a godly woman is described in the book of Proverbs. Proverbs 31 states that a woman is defined as a committed wife to her husband, her physical labor, and her contentment with responsibilities to those who need her (she is not that female who focuses on (me, myself, and I). She can provide for her family and her knowledge in caring for herself to share her strength and knowledge with others. It defines her as an energetic, notable, and multifaceted thoughtful woman who is an individual in her own right. This woman is not branded by her external qualities but by her internal strengths.

When analyzing this emergent scriptural ideal of a godly woman, we do not discover the old-style housewife engaged with a dirty home, her daily life dictated by her spouse and children's demands. Nor do we find a hardened, overly ambitious professional woman who leaves her family to fend for themselves and doesn't have time to spend with God.

With all her responsibilities, first and foremost, what we do find is she is a woman who seeks God, and her primary concern is God's will in her life. She is a woman after God's own heart. She is a woman who wears an abundance of hats, operates with a sacred nature, has an anointing for healing, and is a role model for females seeking to transition into *Godly Womanhood*.

Take a pause and exhale. News flash, girlfriend! The P-31 woman is not to be our idol. God should always be at the forefront of how we live our lives. While it would be fantastic to replicate this superwoman, this is not our ultimate calling. God does not extend that we operate in perfection. Quite frankly, being vulnerable and humble might be a better method. Using your own God-given strength is what God is expecting.

It was several years before I grasped the actual concept of this P-31 woman. I was so busy trying to become every woman. Yes, I'm singing it in my head with my Chaka Khan voice, "I'm every woman." The truth be told, a P-31 woman is constantly evolving. God did not intend us to be every woman, just the one He created us to be. He only allowed His grace so that we could maneuver between multifaceted roles.

The second part of the definition says a woman is a female of the human race grown to adult years. Let's hit that right there! Yes, it confirms there is a process. You are born female but transition into an adult woman. However, there is a difference between the transition from females of this world and what God intends. It is substantially transparent in 1 Corinthians 2:12, "We have not received the spirit of the world but the Spirit who is from God, that we may understand what God has freely given us." And as you continue to dive into the upcoming chapters, I will share my experiences and what thus says the Lord.

"We have not received the spirit of the world but the Spirit who is from God, that we may understand what God has freely given us."
1 Corinthians 2:12
New International Version

In part, the final ingredient, *Wikipedia* describes women in the bible as victors and victims who change the course of historical events and are powerless to affect even their own destinies. This application applies to you today. For you to transition from female to *Godly Womanhood,* there will be seasons of victories, seasons in the valley, seasons where you will feel victimized, and seasons where you will change the course of your family, your culture, your race, and your community. There will also be seasons where you will ingest and endure so much you will reach a vulnerable state of mind, even in your discovery. But God says in Isaiah 41:10, "Don't fear." He promises you that he will be with you always, and he will strengthen you.

"Fear not, for I am with you, be not dismayed for I am your God; I will strengthen you, I will help you, uphold you with my righteous right hand."
Isaiah 41:10
English Standard Version

Several women in the bible parallel my transition as I struggled from female to a godly woman. In John 4:15 KJV, as I reflect on the Samaritan woman at the well when Jesus asked her for a drink of water, she was surprised, as Jews did not associate with Samaritans. Let me paraphrase this story just a bit. The most identifiable and comparable moment in my life is when Jesus corrected the Samaritan woman on the number of husbands throughout her life. She came to the well with an empty bucket (baggage) and had no idea she would be drawing a different kind of water. He offered her the living water that she would never thirst again. Jesus knew what was in her suitcase. He knew of her baggage. When He directed her to go and tell her husband of the living water, the Samaritan woman said she had none. Jesus replied, you are right, you've had five husbands, and the one you're with is not your husband. Well, lick your fingers on that! Jesus was, without a doubt, all in her business.

It is my interpretation that the Samaritan woman reached an evolving moment. Based on the number of husbands, she may have operated in a female mindset.

Understand there is no secret in your life that God cannot already unravel or know. God wants to break every habit you encounter; He intends to quench your thirst so you can be delivered from every stronghold and bad habit you have.

In my worst seasons and three failed marriages over a 12-year period, where I endured physical, emotional, and psychological abuse, Jesus provided me with a breakthrough opportunity. He met me at the well with my female thinking, broken self and offered a business partnership opportunity with all of my baggage. Although my credit was terrible with God, He still opted to give me a loan. To help me get out of debt. All the lousy debt I acquired in those 12 years brought me to a transition point from a female to *Godly Womanhood* and started the journey of who God purposed me to be.

It is imperative to understand your conception is substantial, and you must accept who God created and purposed you to be. In my own experiences, I developed a taste for emerging into womanhood based on people, a man, worldly women, and leaders; it led me to a place of lost identity. These were the symptoms and not the causes of thinking like a female. Many times we treat the symptoms and not the cause. We can't cure what is misdiagnosed. Maybe we are the cause, and we've misdiagnosed someone else or a situation as the cause.

All of that was said to say this! We can't correct what we don't confront. Nothing or anyone in this world will give you the root cause, love, guidance, strength, and endurance to live within your God-given purpose. It is essential not to become a victim of identity theft. We can't allow the world or people in it to dictate our identity. We must value who we are in God and not take His creation lightly. When we don't give credit to God for His marvelous design of us, it is an insult to Him.

God is insistent in His jealousy and requires that while we seek to transition from female to *Godly Womanhood*, He wants you to "Seek the Kingdom of God above all else" (Matthew 6:33, NLT). Subsequently, you will discover His creative ability to transform you, even in the most difficult seasons in your life.

What God sees in you is what no one else will. He is that man who walks around you and checks you out, and sees you from the inside out. God sees you as a jewel; You are the diamond in the rough. You are His rock sculpted into fine art. Humanity will see your flaws, but gospel artist Marvin Sapp says God will see the best in you when everyone else will see the worst in you. Why? Because you are fearfully and wonderfully made to be a godly woman. (Psalms 139:14, ESV)

Girlfriend, I have one more surprise for you; I've invited a guest, who prepared a special treat. We need a man's perspective on his take on a female versus woman, so don't leave the table just yet.

A Man's Point of View

When I was a child, I spake as a child, I understood as a child, I thought as a child: but when I became a man, I put away childish things. (1 Corinthians 13:11, KJV)

A real man is a disciplined male, self-controlled, responsible, and a Lover of God. Thank you for having me, and it is a pleasure to sit at the table with you to give insight from a Man's perspective of a female versus a woman. Like this book's title, my opinion is the same; *Every Man is a Male but not every Male is a Man.* This section is not an exhaustive breakdown but a short perspective of some truths that I hope will give you some food for thought or a different view of seeing things.

First, let me say that I am aware of cultural differences in what some believe and say what and who is a man. For example, some Eastern parts of the world have different views and perspectives on what defines a man. However, I am stating this perspective from a Western Christian point of view. Therefore, the difference between a *Godly Man* versus a male or what is considered a worldly man. Having said that, let's get into it!

I recall discussing love and dating with some teens and young adults years ago. Some of the girls made a statement that invoked agreement with most of the girls in the group. They said, "All Men are Dogs." I'm sure you have heard that statement before or something similar.

I responded, "No," that's not true; you have only dealt with males and not a *Godly Man*. I went on to say, "Every Man is a Male but not Every Male is a Man". It got quiet as they thought about the statement. I went on to explain the difference between the two. I will be sharing that in a moment, as this is the point of this section.

We are all influenced by various factors, where we live, what we see, who we are around, what we have experienced, and what's taught. So when a female makes a statement like, "All Men are Dogs," they have come to a conclusion by either experience or influence. Either a man has dogged them out, or a man mistreated someone they knew or seen.

A man is not a man because of his muscular physique or deep and smooth voice. So when it's time for you to look for a *Godly Man*, a real man, and not just a male, one has to look at the person's complete characteristics and not on the person's outer appearance. Just because he is attractive and appears to have it going on doesn't mean he is a *Godly Man.*

A *Real/Godly Man* has transitioned from being just a male boy into a man. So, what am I saying, you may ask? I am glad that question arose. So, I will briefly tell you what you should be looking for in a *Godly Man* and give you a glimpse of a Man's point of view of what he is looking for in a woman, or rather a *Godly Woman.*

What do I mean by the term *Godly Man* or *Godly Woman?* First, I am not trying to insult anyone by distinguishing the difference between the two. There is a difference, however, when God is involved. A true man of God is different than the males of the world because of his relationship with God.

When I speak of a *Godly Man,* I define someone who has matured from a boy into a man of God.

- ❖ He loves God first.
- ❖ He takes responsibility for his actions and doesn't blame others.
- ❖ He is mature and controlled in his actions and temperament.
- ❖ He is not easily provoked and thinks before he speaks.
- ❖ A *Godly Man* is a mentor, a protector of the innocent, and listens to wise counsel.
- ❖ He is a lover of God and outwardly worships Him.

These are just some of the main characteristics you should look for when looking for a man and not a male.

So, having said all that, you should know what a real man of God looks for in a *Godly Woman.* In the next chapter, I will leave the complete breakdown of the Godly Woman to Minister "Ro" as she will point out more godly woman characteristics, but I want to leave you with a bit of perspective from a man's point of view.

What does a real man of God want and look for in a woman? I am glad you asked. I am speaking from the perspective of a male that has matured into a *Self-Controlled, Disciplined Lover of God.* Likewise, this man is looking for a self-controlled, mature, disciplined woman and lover of God.

Your six-figure salary and nicely shaped body don't mean a thing if you are immature and out of control. A male will entertain females and their mess but will not introduce them to his mother. On the other hand, a man of God looks to introduce this mature Woman of God to his mother and friends.

A man of God wants to come home to a house of peace and not contention. A man of God is looking for a woman to support their dreams together. A man of God is looking for the female that has become a *Godly Woman.* How you carry yourself is essential. Do you have moral standards that you live by and teach your children?

A real man of God is looking for a woman that will be a good nurturing mother to their children. She is humble and shows compassion and hospitality to others. She is kind, respective, and respected.

Though she is not perfect, she has learned that over time and experience, she has matured to become the woman God has called her to be. Ultimately, this is what a real man of God is looking for in a *Godly Woman.*

When both male and female become a *Godly Man* and *Godly Woman*, the possibilities to be used by God impact each other and others become endless.

Pastor Glen Robertson- Sin4no1ministries

Okay, girlfriend, let's keep it moving; let me ask you a few questions to lead you into the next chapter. How do you define your womanhood? Are you living your life with godly womanhood principles? What are those principles? (note 2) to Before you turn to the next chapter, write these questions down and answer them. Then, you will be able to match them up with a few women in the bible and determine if you are defining your *Godly Womanhood* based on societal terms or godly terms. Are you ready? Let's go!

NOTE 2

My Devotional Thoughts

How do you define your *Godly Womanhood*? Are you living your life with any godly womanhood principles? If so, what are those principles?

____

____

____

____

____

____

____

____

____

____

____

____

Prayer

Heavenly Father, I come before you seeking to be made whole. I pray You to unclog my spiritual ears to hear Your voice and give me the discernment to know the difference. Open my eyes to the benefits of the process so that I may reach a spiritual evolution about who You called me to be. I desire to understand the difference between being a female and a woman. May the process from female to Godly Womanhood reveal who I am. Create a clean heart and a renewed mind in me so I may transform into Your likeness. Amen

Scripture of Meditation

"God is within her; she will not fall; God will help her at break of day." (Psalms 46:5, NIV)

"I praise you because I am fearfully and wonderfully made; your works are wonderful; I know that full well." (Psalms 139:14, NIV)

"For as the woman originated from the man, so also the man has his birth through the woman; and all things originate from God." (1 Corinthians 11:12, NASB)

"But by the grace of God, I am what I am, and His grace to me was not without effect. No, I worked harder than all of them—yet not I, but the grace of God that was with me." (1 Corinthians 15:10, NIV)

"Blessed is she who has believed that the Lord would fulfill his promises to her!" (Luke 1:45, NIV)

"Similarly, teach the older women to live in a way that honors God. They must not slander others or be heavy drinkers. Instead, they should teach others what is good." (Titus 2:3-5, NLT)

CHAPTER THREE

GODLY WOMANHOOD

"God is in the midst of her, and she shall not be moved."

Psalms 46:5 (NKJV)

Welcome girlfriend to the campfire, grab a seat, and let's chat about this perspective called *Godly Womanhood*. Quick question? When did you decide that you were a woman? Was it when you experienced your first kiss or maybe your first boyfriend, Mr. Delicious, came into your life, was it when you lost your virginity, or perhaps when you moved out of your parents' house for the very first time? Did you finally meet your Boaz, marry him, and have a few kids? Wait! There it is, you turned 40. Oh, yea! That's it, and now you have fully embraced *Godly Womanhood*. If that's your story, let me put some more wood on the fire, we might be here longer than expected. We're going to camp out in this section and peel back some more layers.

Did you know experiencing all those things doesn't place you in a godly woman category? Sex, money, becoming a boss lady or a wife, entrepreneurship, beauty, having a man, or not even going to church every Sunday can define you as a mature, godly woman.

I remember the first thought of solidifying my *Godly Womanhood,* and it was after becoming pregnant and giving birth to my first child. In my mind, giving life to another human being meant that I'd reached total and complete womanhood capacity. I was married, paying my bills, working every day, and there wasn't anyone who could convince me otherwise. Little did I know, I was nowhere close to *Godly Womanhood.* I was insecure, had daddy and mommy issues, little girl syndrome, and feared the entire world. I had what I called imposter syndrome! Everything looked real good from the outside. I was pretending to be something I was not. The fake smile, dressed to the T, appeared to be well to do and put together. But when the layers were peeled back, my gosh. I know I'm all by myself on this thing, right! Externally it wasn't visible, but I was suffering from internal bleeding and struggled to connect with my own true identity on the inside. Does this sound familiar?

As I grew older, my poor vision turned into glaucoma, and my addiction moved from coffee and tea to perfection and approval. I was even more unclear about *Godly Womanhood*. By the time I reached 30, I was already in my third marriage and my third child. The struggle was real, and I was so far away from who God purposed me to be. I found myself changing directions constantly, jobs, relationships, and churches, hoping each change would give me peace or fill the emptiness in my heart. I kept thinking that it would get better this time, it would be different, but it only got worse. I lacked purpose because I could not identify a sense of self, value, or *Godly Womanhood*. I was in complete rejection of who God ordained me to be. And get this, I was introduced to God even before He met me at the well, but I had no relationship with him.

Let me toss this nugget. Get ready. Catch! When you reject or deny your God-ordained identity and uniqueness, you lessen Holy Spirit's ability to operate in you entirely. Holy Spirit is a comforter, and He will not move beyond your comfort zone or pass how you embrace yourself. Your regard for who you are in Him is essential to the Holy Spirit's natural glory and power. Therefore, I decree you will reach a revelation to learn to embrace, love, and honor you regardless of what others think, validate, or regard you.

After thousands of mistakes, chaos, and seasons of heartache, I truly felt everything but like a godly woman. Later in the chapters, I'll be more naked about those seasons. I know you are probably asking how much more naked can I get! But for now, let's add another log to the fire and talk about biblical principles of *Godly Womanhood* and what God expects.

The biblical description of a godly woman gave a foundation for *Godly Womanhood,* and it laid out a very distinctive character when it comes to a woman in the bible. When God created man and woman, he designed women to think differently, process emotions, and make decisions differently. But yet, men and women are made to complement each other. Now isn't that something! I'm having an oh, hum, moment as I'm writing this! In my thought process, I related to Steve Harvey's book, "Act Like a Lady Think Like a Man."

You know that saying, men are from mars and women are from Venus? Well, there might be some truth to this, ha-ha! A woman encompasses no attributes of a man because she can never be a man. A man can never contain the characteristics of a woman because he can never be a woman. However, I've had a season where I've felt like I had to not just think like a man but operate in the actions of a man. The epiphany hit me! That's why I was tired all the time. Trying to play both roles of man and woman is exhausting. God made it clear he wanted a woman to stay in her lane.

God will sometimes position you in the assignment that a man fills typically, but it doesn't require you to forsake your *Godly Womanhood* role. If I could emulate myself as a woman character in the bible, it is Deborah. She has an impressive resume and is one of the baddest and most influential chicks in the bible. As a judge and a prophet, she was known to hear God's voice and share God's Word with others. As a priestess, she did not offer sacrifices as the men did, but she was a dynamic worship leader and preacher. She was a worshiping warrior and found encouragement and strength in worship to be obedient to everything the Lord was asking her to do. God placed Deborah in the assignment, typically that of a man as judge and warrior, but she did not forsake her *Godly Womanhood*. (Judges 4)

Deborah did it big when it came to God. If she had played it small in her life, Deborah would not have encountered all the experiences that led to being used by the Lord.

Finding your journey to biblical *Godly Womanhood* starts and ends with Christ Jesus. Therefore, you have the responsibility to obey and serve God. Yes, you were born female, but you must be born again to transition from a female to a godly woman. I don't mean physically born again; I am talking about being spiritually born again.

There must be a spiritual awakening. We are not sinners because we do wrong, but choose wrong because we are sinners! No matter how many good deeds we do, we can not change our nature. We have to be transformed from within by God.

Everything you are wrestling against to define your *Godly Womanhood* is spiritual. You are under spiritual attack because the enemy knows once you discover your true identity to *Godly Womanhood*, you will be tenacious, planted, unmovable, and simply unstoppable.

All those broken pieces you keep pulling out of your junk box in the back of your closet to define your identity are what the enemy wants you to use to create the narrative about who you are. I kept pulling out all that junk from my childhood, the rape, the molestation, parental neglect, and the abuse, to piece together a woman's identity of myself. I remember looking at every woman around me, trying to mimic what kind of woman I was supposed to become. Some of those very same women I wanted to be seated at the table with did not have my best interest. There were at least two Judas at the table. (The Book of Acts) All of these frenemies were looking for opportunities for me to crash and burn.

The wheel belongs to God! When you compromise your authenticity to be seated at a table with those you believe to be influential, you risk compromising your identity. You blend yourself for a seat with the ungodly and risk eating spoiled food. God will reposition your heart and call you to His table. However, he won't force-feed you. Instead, if you choose to partake of His bread and partner with Him, He will navigate your position or situation and drive you right to the destination of *Godly Womanhood.*

When you compromise your authenticity to be seated at a table with those you believe to be influential, you risk compromising your identity.

It took me to develop a deep transparent relationship with God and be born again, to realize that even my mother could not truly define my *Godly Womanhood.*

And this is not to say there were no influential women in my life. There were several, but God wanted me to have a divine alignment with Him.

If you want to invoke God's power in your life or situation, you must build a relationship with Him. We will take all the time and put all our effort into worldly relationships but want to evoke God's authority in our situation without knowing who He is. And expect to receive blessings through Him. Would it not be an insult if someone showed up at your door and started asking you for things, and you didn't know who they were. God is no different; He is not cheap and wants us to see the value of who He is. However, it would help if you disposed of some stuff to build that relationship.

Girlfriend, I want you to take everything out of your junk box, crushing your spirit and hindering you from the process into *Godly Womanhood and building a relationship with God.* Write it down, and throw it into the fire (note 3). Then, I need you to cast all your cares upon the Lord. After a while, it starts to stink if you don't clean out your junk box. And every time you pull something out of it, that funky smell becomes attached to you. So, you'll walk around with a smelly female attitude, with old wounds, and adopting characteristics from people who may be on an assignment from the enemy to crush what God has planted inside of you. In other words, keep your temple clean and rid of everything so that the Lord does not turn away from you. (Deuteronomy 23:14, NIV)

***For For the LORD your God moves about in your camp
to protect you and to deliver your enemies to you.
Your camp must be holy so that he will not see among
you anything indecent and turn away from you.***
Deuteronomy 23:14
New International Version

Alright, girlfriend, get your bibles out; let's navigate to John 3:3, where it says Jesus replied, "Very truly I tell you, no one can see the kingdom of God unless they are born again." You have read it for yourself, and the bible gives clear instructions. If you read further in the scripture, in John 3:3, Jesus clarifies the meaning of being born again. "Flesh gives birth to flesh, but the Spirit gives birth to spirit." So, stepping out of your fleshly female spirit and embracing Godly Womanhood begins with you being born again. It will help if you become a "new creature in Christ Jesus" (2 Corinthians 5:17, NJV). When you are born again, your level of intimacy with God will increase.

To be intimate with God, you must surrender yourself and allow your old ways and identity to die. You must submit your fleshly self for His Spirit to dwell within you. God wants to resurrect us so that we become that godly woman we desire. Eventually, you will need to get past the boyfriend stage and seek a higher level. Girlfriend! The Bride Groom awaits your presence!

Unless we are born again, it's hard to transition out of some seasons. We get out of the season, but the season doesn't get out of us. We should be born again to reach a "spiritual rebirth" or a regeneration of our human spirit and reach a cleansing that only God can do. If we admit we are stinky, unclean, our actions are ungodly, and we ask for forgiveness of our sins, God says, "I will give you a new heart and put a new spirit within you" (Ezekiel 36:26, NLT). God is so awesome; He gives us a new purpose and new goals for living. We began to have a new strut and dance, put on our clothes differently, and speak a new language because His blood washes us clean. It moves us away from sin and closer to God.

And I will give you a new heart, and I will put a new spirit in you. I will take out your stony, stubborn heart and give you a tender, responsive heart.
Ezekiel 36:26
New Living Translation

If you are intentional about your transition from female to *Godly Womanhood*, you must take Jesus's words seriously and abide in Him. Let the Word of God be the final authority in your life. Without His authority, the spiritual warfare and battle with *Godly Womanhood* are like a tree that bears no fruit. (John 15:5, NIV)

"I am the vine; you are the branches. If you remain in me and I in you, you will bear much fruit; apart from me, you can do nothing."
John 15:5
New International Version

When I explained the female attributes in the earlier chapter, it was clear that mindset can get you caught up in a cage. I don't mean literally or physically being in a cage but spiritually, emotionally, or mentally bound to a cage. It keeps you from spiritual revelation. You will be so wrapped in worldly depictions that it will keep you blinded, and you will lose sight of pursuing your dreams and developing your gifts. Therefore, before I move to the next section, I want you to decree and declare the following:

I am sold out for Jesus! He is the lover of my soul. He brings me joy amid my circumstances, guides my feet when stumbling, and loves me through my transgressions. He dances with me during the midnight hours; He never talks behind my back. He gives me the truth; I love Him more than anything. He says He will wait for me and wants to share an eternity with me.

God's standard for *Godly Womanhood*

Your external beauty is not relevant to God's standard for you to meet His expectations of *Godly Womanhood*. Therefore, standard number one is in first

Peter 3:3-4, which says, "Your beauty should not come from outward adornments, such as elaborate hairstyles and the wearing of gold jewelry or fine clothes. Rather, it should be that of your inner self, the unfading beauty of a gentle and quiet spirit, which is of great worth in God's sight."

A female allows herself to be identified by her outer representation of qualities and beauty. She caters to what society or others expect. She has no sight of her worth and value. And does everything in her power to create herself into something other than what God created her to be.

Girlfriend, don't trip! Let's take another pause! I'm not indicating you are not to take care of yourselves. What I am saying is, don't let your beauty become you're idle based on societal standards.

I don't think there is anywhere in the Bible where God lays out this same standard for a man. I believe God fully understands what He has created for a godly woman. God is watching everything you do as a female. He knew you would use your body to gain favor over men, use your charm to persuade another woman's husband, gain material possession or sleep your way to the top level on that job. So don't exploit your outer appearance for worldly things, people, or possessions. God wants you to know your natural beauty is found in His reflection, both physically and internally.

There is that old saying, beauty is only skin deep! You can be gorgeous as a barbie doll on the outside and be a dark knight on the inside. But, if you apply the principles of biblical womanhood, you'll begin to experience a tender and gentler spirit. When you allow the Holy Spirit to guide you, God will bless your natural giftings and use your inner core, so doors will be open that you couldn't even imagine.

I want to encourage you if you are reading this and are at a crossroads of your identity. Understand that God loves you, and His glory is unique to each person, especially the female gender. I want you to know that your identity is in the image and recognition of God. He designed women to reflect specific aspects of His glory through *Godly Womanhood*.

The fire is burning out, girlfriend. So let's wrap this conversation up. Get some rest, and don't forget to check in tomorrow.

NOTE 3

My Devotional Thoughts

Girlfriend, I want you to take everything out of your junk box, crushing your spirit and hindering you from the process into *Godly Womanhood* and building a relationship with God. Write it down, and throw it into the fire. Then, I need you to cast all your cares upon the Lord.

____

____

____

____

____

____

____

____

____

____

____

____

____

Prayer

Lord, You know my heart better than any other. You know what I believe and what I don't believe. You know my character, strengths and weaknesses, and everything about me, even every thought. Please help me to understand myself. Would You please help me come to a complete understanding of you firmly? Never let me turn my back on You. Help me see You are the truth to the Godly Womanhood I seek. In Jesus' Name, Amen

Scriptures of Meditation

"An excellent wife, who can find? For her worth is far above jewel." (Proverbs 31:10, NASB)

"She is more precious than jewels, And nothing you desire compares with her." (Proverbs 3:15, NASB)

"She looks well to the ways of her household and does not eat the bread of idleness." (Proverbs 31:27, NASB)

*"For women who claim to be devoted to God should make themselves attractive by the good things they do."
(1 Timothy 2:10, NLT)*

"She opens her mouth in wisdom, And the teaching of kindness is on her tongue." (Proverbs 31:26, NASB)

"The wise woman builds her house, But the foolish tears it down with her own hands." (Proverbs 14:1, NASB)

CHAPTER FOUR

CREATED FOR A PURPOSE

"God has a purpose behind every problem. He uses circumstances to develop our character. In fact, He depends more on circumstances to make us like Jesus than he depends on our reading the bible."

Rick Warren

It's a gift basket fellowship; this basket has a different set of life instructions for you. The items from this basket are essential in your process from female to *Godly Womanhood.* It will take some time to get through them all, so kick off your shoes, make yourself comfortable, and let's jump right into it. Your purpose is within you, and you are the basket that is magnificently woven together by God's hands.

He works all things, including your life, according to His purpose. (Romans 8:28, NIV)

So, I'm reaching inside the basket of life, and I've pulled out the biblical definition of "Purposeful Living," according to *faithward.org,* which declares why you exist. "It is a structured and scripture-based process to find your calling from God and fulfill your God-given purpose. This process will guide you toward answers to foundational questions, like: "Who is God shaping me to be?" and "What is God preparing me to do?" so that you can fulfill your calling from God." It captures the heart of why you are on this earth and why Jesus died for you. It defines your life—not in terms of what you think but what God thinks. It anchors your life in the character and call of God.

Often, when in a chaotic environment, it's hard to filter through how to define your purpose. You can become so entangled in what and who is around you your vision becomes obscured. You end up on journeys in life that are nowhere near where God purposed you to be. The noise is so loud; that you can become distracted or deaf and lose your hearing of God's voice.

Distraction comes in all forms and from all directions, but the result is the same each time. Distraction takes us off course, and it either prevents us from experiencing something God has for us or puts us in the wrong position. Getting back on track from being spiritually distracted isn't tricky but requires us to be intentional with our time and attention.

Let me take you back to Eden for a moment. Remember Eve? I mentioned her in the garden. She had everything;

it was like being in a utopia. But unfortunately, the serpent was able to distract Eve when she was isolated. I'm watching you, girlfriend! You are beginning to use your fan. Is it getting a little hot in the room? Let me hit that thermostat because the temperature will rise a bit more.

Let me dig deep into one of these baskets and see what else I can pull out! Well, let's see what this is! It looks like community and prayer are at the top of the basket.

Community helps drive your purpose. So, you will need intercessory prayer warriors, godly influences, and sometimes downright counseling to get back on track. Here is why you will need community influence; one, the kingdom of God operates in timing. So often, we are impatient and don't wait on God to impart in our lives what we need. Girlfriend, you know what I mean, slick Ricky will slide right on up in there, and in the blink of an eye, you're in a marriage from hell. You let Boaz slip right by you because he didn't fit the status quo, was not street enough, and wanted to wait to be married before sex. The enemy will become an influence that will get us to act too soon or not soon enough out of fear and insecurity.

The second thing is that the enemy will appear like the devil in a blue dress. They may look and act normal, but there is a hidden agenda. This devil can perpetuate a good friend or even a godly man. What appears in them is not who they are or say they are. And before you know it, you are caught up in a whirled win and wonder how you got hoodwinked. This overwhelming pressure makes you feel like you can't breathe and feel anxious and excited.

You know when the pressure starts because you feel like you are being squeezed in the middle seat of an airplane between big Tommy and a sumo wrestler. Then bam! What you thought was going to be is really not. Well, news flash, it's the enemy setting you up; it's a counterfeit! It will look like that perfect job, the ideal relationship, or the ideal outcome. But there is a caveat involved; these things will include a compromise like dating slick Ricky or taking a career position that moves you further away from your purpose. So now you are making moves to get yourself out of a situation.

Just remember we are the treasure hidden in a jar of clay, and when we are hard pressed on every side of life, we will not be crushed, perplexed, and not in despair. We may even feel persecuted, but we will never be abandoned or struck down. (2 Corinthians 4;7-9, NIV)

I spent my 20's, 30's, and some of my 40's living under my terms and leaning on my own strength. And yes, I am mentioning it again; I purposed myself in people, money, jobs, things, marriages, and even sex. It was all due to no clear comprehension of variance between the mindset of a female and *Godly Womanhood.*

Everything I did, every decision I made, was driven by a female approach and lacked divine purpose. Yes, I was that female purposed in tendencies driven by the flesh. But something in my spirit was screaming to be transitioned into a godly purposed woman who had propensities guided by the principles of God. So look what else I pulled out of the basket, Romans 12:2, which says, do not conform to this world!

Do not conform to the pattern of this world, but be transformed by the renewing of your mind. Then you will be able to test and approve what God's will is his good, pleasing and perfect will."
Romans 12:2
New International Version

I want to toss in another nugget, so listen, who God purposed you to be is non-negotiable. God's word never changes, and it's evident in defining who He created you to be, regardless of your circumstances. Therefore, operating in a female mindset did not take away what God purposed in you. In other words, you must be deliberate about seeking God for clarity of your purpose. In all the poor decisions, the environment that shapes your testimony, through all your heartaches, and your childhood wounds. God will keep His promise despite societal norms or how others have associated you with these life-altering experiences. He declares that if you ask, it will be given to you; seek, and you will find; knock, and it will be opened to you. (Mathew 7:7, ESV)

Are you identifying with this chapter so far? If not, are you experiencing the feeling of just existing without direction or foundation? Is there no joy or excitement in your life? Do you feel stuck or unfulfilled no matter what you do?

You're just existing and not living; you've fallen and can't get up; you're looking to turn your bitterness into betterness and don't know-how. Or you feel like an outcast. You've worn a mask to cover up your brokenness; You are addicted to financial prosperity. You've married or sought relationships for a feeling of wholeness, yet you still feel inadequate and wonder why. It's because none of it will ever make you think you are living a purposeful life; it's all bogus. So, I have to go in on you just a bit.

Let me give you a reality check, impulsive shopping for relationships will not give you eternal life. It's a temporary feel-good moment, and people or money will not provide you with access to the heavenly kingdom. It just satisfies your empty emotion and your flesh. The promotion you thought would position you for greatness took you further away from where God needed you to be. And that good sex you were having was only a temporary fix, and using what's between your legs will never fix your emptiness. The numerous men you've married will not give you the feeling of purpose like God can. None of these continuous actions help you transition from female to *Godly Womanhood* or get you any closer to your goal.

Please understand my thoughts on this. I'm not saying that seeking promotion, marriage, financial prosperity, and shopping for things are wrong. On the contrary, God does want you to prosper. Let me put it more into context; I don't want to mislead you, so let's let the word speak for itself. The bible is clear, "But seek first his kingdom and his righteousness, and all these things will be given to you as well." (Matthew 6:33, NIV). It's when those things become your idle that becomes an issue.

When you focus your thoughts on heavenly things, everything you desire that aligns with God's purpose will be provided to you. So, if you feel stuck, on your job, in your marriage, fighting with low self-esteem, worldly temptation, depressed or feeling inadequate, I want to encourage you to go to your bible and hook up with this spiritual brother name Paul. He wrote the book of Colossians, and he wanted me to remind you to start setting your minds on things above, not on things of this earth (Colossians 3:2, NIV). And watch the process of change from a female to *Godly Womanhood* begin.

"Set your mind on things above, not on earthly things, for you died, and your life is now hidden with Christ in God. When Christ, who is your life, appears, then you also will appear with him in glory. Put to death, therefore, whatever belongs to your earthy nature."
Colossians 3:2-17
New International Version

When I look back on those 20 through 40 years of my life, I was so busy *"doing"* that there was no room for *"being."* When I was torn up from the floor up and limping back to God, I realized how far I was from my purpose. Those seasons in my life clarified who God has shaped me to be today. If I haven't said it enough, understanding who God is will prepare you to discover and pursue God's vision for your life.

I see something blinking at the bottom of this golden basket. Wow, it's restoration! Yes, girlfriend, God is a restorer, and when He restores, it is always better than it was initially. God's promise is a better way, a better life, and a better future. He will take everything broken in you, fill it with His blood, put it back together again, and make it 100 percent better than it was before. So, please raise your reclined seat on this one to be very attentive to what I am getting ready to say.

Whatever the enemy has snatched from you, God wants to restore it and make it better for you. Understand every day; we have choices that will come before us. We can be tempted to be hurt, depressed, stuck in a cage, wounded, or even complain and stay in this state of mind. Or we can seek to partner with God and be in pursuit of a purpose-driven life. And watch the work of restoration begin.

Please write down everything you hear the Lord is saying to you about your purposed life. And everything the devil is attacking in your life to keep you from a purposeful life. (Note 4) Then, at the end of this chapter, let's break some yokes and bind these assignments over your life.

Pursuit of a Purpose Driven Life

Let's dig deeper into this basket of life for a more profound methodology and discover the benefits of operating with a purpose-driven life. You might find the following statement a bit of a surprise; wait for it..........! Well, here it comes! Your purpose isn't always about you.

In his book the Purpose Driven Life, Pastor Rick Warren says, "The greatest tragedy is not death, but life without purpose." Therefore, remember earlier, in the pursuit of purpose, I noted that the further I was away from God, the closer I was to sin. Let me provide a more descriptive layout for you. The Israelites were a nation of people that God freed from bondage, and because of their sin and disobedience, they wandered in the wilderness for 40 years, not accepting God's purpose over their lives.

The closer you are to God, the closer you are to your purpose, and the further away you are to God, the further you are away from your purpose. Ouch! Yes, it is painful to hear, but the truth will give you the freedom to govern your choices in line with living a purpose-driven life.

The closer you are to God, the closer you are to your purpose, and the further away you are to God, the further you are away from your purpose.

Let's get back to the phrase; the purpose isn't always about you. God will always order the steps of the godly (Psalms 37:23, NLT). Your status on this earth does not define your purpose. It's not defined by your job, how many titles or degrees you have, your mother or father, your husband, your children, or the amount of wealth you have. When God gives you purpose, it's used for His glory. For example, you may think you are in a high-level position to gain more authority or prestige. However, God may have placed you on an assignment as a leader or facilitator who is to demonstrate an example of leading with a kingdom mindset, but you are fighting against it.

On the other hand, if you surrender, God may be positioning you to be a reflection of Him, showing others how to lead with a servant's heart. If you walk in His season or plan, He is sure to use it to benefit promotion, earthly and kingdom promotion. Think about it! Accepting God's plan has opened doors to teaching and speaking engagements across your industry about better ways to facilitate. Sometimes the very thing you are fighting against is the same thing that God uses to thrust you into what you're purposed to do.

God intends for every female to reach a place of revelation. What He starts, He will finish. God will continue to do good work in you if you yield to Him.

The basket is almost empty, but one thing is left at the bottom of your basket. So please take a few moments and pull it out. Yes, it's your purpose-driven kit! It includes everything you need to be restored, delivered, renewed, and empowered to move from un-purposed to purposed. I declare you will be that godly woman God created you to be. Read this daily along with your end chapter prayer.

Purposed for His plans
Jeremiah 29:11

Unified with His spirit
John 14:26

Redeemed by His blood
Ephesians 1:7

Prepared for the battle
Philippians 4:13

Obedient to His will
Psalms 128:1

Saved by His grace
Psalms 128:1

Exalt Him for His power
Psalms 21:13

NOTE 4

My Devotional Thoughts

Please write down everything you hear the Lord is saying to you about your purposed life. And everything where the devil is attacking you in your life, keeping you from a purposeful life.

____

____

____

____

____

____

____

____

____

____

____

Prayer

Heavenly Father, thank You for the grace and mercy bestowed upon me. I give You thanks and praise for Your powerful Holy Spirit within me working to fulfill your will and purpose in my life. I humbly ask that You teach me how to effectively partner with Your Spirit to hear from You and know Your choice for my life. In so doing, I will be transformed by renewing my mind and receiving the fullness of my inheritance in You. Forgive me for all the choices that have kept me from partnering with You. Please help me with my weaknesses. Teach me to trust You because You said in Your word that Your strength is made perfect in my weakness. And Lord, I ask You to help me remember that when I pray the Spiritual gifts and purpose over my life, I will be empowered daily to live a purposeful Christ-like life and overcome the power of Satan and the lusts of the flesh. In Jesus' Name, Amen

Scriptures of Meditation

"Many are the plans in a person's heart, but it is the Lord's purpose that prevails." (Proverbs 19:21, NIV)

"The purposes of a person's heart are deep waters, but one who has insight draws them out." (Proverbs 20:5, NIV)

"I know that you can do all things; no purpose of yours can be thwarted." (Job 42:2, NIV)

"Therefore, my dear friends, as you have always obeyed not only in my presence but now much more in my absence—continue to work out your salvation with fear and trembling, for it is God who works in you to will and to act in order to fulfill his good purpose." (Philippians 2:12-13, NIV)

"And we know that in all things God works for the good of those who love him, who have been called according to his purpose." (Romans 8:28, NIV)

"For you have been called for this purpose, since Christ also suffered for you, leaving you an example for you to follow in His steps." (1 Peter 2:21, NIV)

"But have nothing to do with worldly fables fit only for old women. On the other hand, discipline yourself for the purpose of godliness." (1 Timothy 4:7, NIV)

CHAPTER FIVE

ACCEPTANCE

*Grace is God's acceptance of us. Faith is
our acceptance of God accepting us."*

Adrian Rogers

Today is reflection day! Please get your mirror out and look deeply into it. Do you see the female or the godly woman or a little bit of both? Now ask yourself, do you love who you are? Do you accept all your personality traits and physical attributes? The sagging boobs, your dark or light skin. Are you critical of your hair, or maybe you're critical of your height? Do you think you are too tall or too short? Do you see someone wounded, hurt, or too critical of themselves? You might find that you stutter when you speak or learn differently. Do you accept every part of your flaws and all of you? If the answer is no, you've got some pruning to do. Acceptance starts with pruning back all the dead leaves so you can blossom into your full potential.

To reach a place of wholeness, self-resilience, and acceptance, you must ditch the female characteristics and submit to God's creation.

Acceptance is an action; it is the result of the process of contending with, wrestling it out in prayer, fasting, repenting, and finally yielding to His higher purpose for your life. It believes that "all things are possible" (Mark 10:27, KJV).

Everything you don't accept about yourself causes you to carry doubt about your creation. You twist yourself into something or somebody else because you don't like God's creation. As a result, you spend the bulk of your time fitting in to get in. Believe it when I say God created you to be radical; He set you apart to be different, unique, and one of a kind.

When you discard or reject your God-ordained identity and distinctiveness, you diminish the Holy Spirits' opportunity to work the transition in you entirely. Yes, I'm preaching it again! You must stay faithful to His direction over your life. Don't venture out to satisfy your flesh or someone else's suggestion. And don't allow persecution, past hurts, and criticisms to push you back into the cage. Instead, as you build a closer relationship with God, begin to build a resistance to your negative thoughts or people. Guard your heart and let God lead you with his spirit and words until there is no trace of the female or propulsion within you.

Don't venture out to satisfy your flesh or someone else's suggestion. And don't allow persecution, past hurts, and criticisms to push you back into the cage.

Listen, your imperfections were part of God's plan. When you don't recognize or accept who you are, it pulls you further from the woman and closer to the female. Would you please take a few minutes and affirm your existence in 1 Peter 2:9?

"But you are a chosen race, a royal priesthood, a holy nation, a people for God's own possession, so that you may proclaim the excellencies of Him who has called you out of darkness into His marvelous light;"
1 Peter 2:9
New American Standard Bible

In my Patty Lebelle voice, it says, "The Best is Yet to come." He made you wonderfully complex, and His workmanship is marvelous. He watched you as you were being formed in utter isolation, as you were interlaced together in the dim of the womb. He saw you before you were born" (Psalms 139:13-16). Each day of your life recorded in His book is laid out before a single day has passed. In other words, girl, God thinks you got it going on!

One of the valuable things in your transition from Female to *Godly Womanhood* is forgiving yourself. Forgiveness is truly a gift from God, and He intended us to utilize this gift to walk in His image. The message in His word tells us that God forgives us, and He took the punishment for the wrong things we have done. However, despite God's message, we often find it difficult to forgive, especially ourselves.

I believe forgiveness begins with two things acknowledgment and acceptance. First, we must acknowledge those things that keep us operating in a female state of mind. We must identify all the enablers of our stagnation, anger, bitterness, self-doubt, and hurt, including ourselves. Second, we must acknowledge the problematic perplexities in our lives, as challenging as they may seem, which have contributed to our behaviors, poor relationships, addictions, and life choices. Sometimes we do have to look back to move forward.

Bridging the gap between acknowledgment, acceptance, and forgiveness is imminent to your deliverance and transition from female to *Godly Womanhood*. They are like the three amigos and are the three-fold cord that moves us into a place of wholeness.

To get to a place of acceptance, you must be willing to do something you've never done. When God takes something from your grasp, He is not punishing you but merely opening your hands to receive something spectacular. So concentrate on this sentence, "The will of God will never take you where the grace of God will not protect you."

***The will of God will never take you where
the grace of God will not protect you***

Have you ever been fascinated about doing something, visiting a specific location, or achieving a specific goal? Do you want to arrive at that place or accomplish that goal without taking the necessary steps? Do you provide a lot of lip service, but your actions don't match up, or faith doesn't add up, or trust in God doesn't match up, but you are expecting a great outcome? Reality check, lip service alone doesn't accomplish much. If this is you, your reflection in the mirror probably reflects that of a female?

The bible says, whatever you do, work whole heartily (Colossians 3:23-24, ESV). So, I'm saying, girlfriend, you must put in some work. The most important thing you must do is start the journey to arrive at any destination! Listen to this; it is not essential if you know how to get there or not! Just begin the journey. You are halfway there; you have prayed for a renewed spirit, and God has permitted you to pivot so you can prevail.

"Whatever you do work whole heartily as for the Lord not for man, knowing from the Lord you will receive your inheritance and your reward."
Colossians 3:23-24
English Standard Version

Now go back to the mirror, and let's do this again. Come on, girlfriend! Speak life into your spirit. Repeat these words; I have supernatural grace, I am ordained and sanctified by God, and I cannot be disqualified by my physical appearance, mistakes, or addictions. He created me for a purpose, and nothing in life can cause me to be disqualified by God. So, say it loud with a James Brown voice; I am a godly woman, and I'm proud.

If you want to find the road to acceptance, you will need to step out of your box. What does it mean to step outside the box? Well! Stepping outside the box does not mean that you live inside a box, not literary. Everyone lives in a box to some extent. Being in the box refers to what you consider normal or safe. It is your view of life. That easy way you have always known as routine.

You love the comfort of your life, right! What you are used to and familiar with within your everyday environment. Stepping out of the box feels scary, even risky. Life is comfortable when you are inside the box because nothing is strange. However, you may fail to see the adverse effects of the box. The box holds you back. It denies you many blessings and opportunities. It prevents you from exploring God's path and keeps you from reaching your destination because you only see within the perimeters of your box.

The people of Israel were comfortable with being in the wilderness to the point of complaining and murmuring about going back to imprisonment (Exodus 16). Being in the wilderness was outside of their box. The problem is they brought the box mentality with them to the wilderness.

If you find yourself uncomfortable, nervous, stressed, or anxious along the path of accepting your purpose or who you are, it's because you have chosen to step out of your box. For example, there were many obstacles to the Israelites' destination to the Promised Land. As a result, they must have felt a sense of discomfort and uncertainty; even Moses began to cry out to God.

In the book of Exodus, the Lord spoke to Moses and asked, "why are you crying out to me? Tell the people to get moving." He needs Moses to put faith into action. Therefore, if we plan to move from female to *Godly Womanhood,* we must keep progressing ahead with trust and reliance on the Lord.

There must be an incubation period for greatness to form before He transforms you or exposes you. God hides what He has called to mobilize. He leads us in the wilderness so we can go beyond our narcissistic views. And will hide you in the deepest of pain, the darkest valley, and the hottest pit of fire. But when He exposes you, there will be no doubt that He is Lord of your life.

God always hears our cries when we are in bondage. He may not release us when we are ready, but He releases us in His timing. So, God never promised us that life on earth would be created around a bed of roses, but He did say that there is a season and time for every activity under heaven (Ecclesiastics 3:1, NLT). And He also said to be anxious about nothing, but we are to pray about everything(Philippians 4:6, NKJV).

To reach your point of destination, goals, vision, purpose, and promised land, you must be willing not just to take a peek or cry out from the inside of the box but jump out of the box with both feet planted. It is insane to think that you can cry out to God without taking a step forward. Albert Einstein says, "Insanity is doing the same thing repeatedly and expecting a different result." So, if you keep peeking and crying out from the inside of the box, don't expect a different result.

Get Ready!

A new direction is required, so as you look in the mirror, get ready for new territory and a season of awakening to a new standard of accountability, holiness, love, and power. God wants you to prepare for the transition, transformation, and unknown territory.

First, there are going to be some things you have to do once you receive the direction. And second, there will be some things you must do to possess your blessings and new assignments, your calling/purpose, your victory, and the increase to enlarge your territory. Are you ready! Get your Windex out, clean off your mirror and refocus. Alright! Let's get it going!

Turn your mirror to the right and reposition your mindset, attitudes, and thinking. You must have a purposeful and victorious mindset because you are called to be a mover and shaker, a cultural activator, and an atmosphere shifter, but you must stay hungry for the Lord and His voice! You must have bold obedience and an expectant attitude. You must remain pregnant until God is ready for you to go into labor to push out what is coming in the new season.

Turn your mirror to the left and re-examine your faith. Without faith, it is impossible to transition, receive a transformation, or new territory from God. Not all those who left Egypt made it into God's promised land. There will be some folks who were with you in the old season that won't be going with you in your new season. But, it's all good; get your face towel, wipe the tears from your eyes, clean your face and get ready for it.

Your faith can't be grounded in folks you used to hang out with. Your faith is a gift from God, not because you deserve it, have earned it, are worthy of it, or someone gave it to you. You have it because God gave it to you and His grace and mercy. Faith is what will sustain you through the transition and transformation. (Ephesians 2:8-9, ESV)

Reposition the mirror back straight and change up your gear. You can't go into battle being cute; you have to take off the soft shoes, pill off those eyelashes, loosen up that weave, and put on your combat boots.

You have to take off the jacket of hurt and offense, take off the shirt of blame, and remove the people pleaser pants. You have to strip off the garments of haters and naysayers and put on the whole armor of God, and you will be able to stand. (Ephesians 6:11, NIV)

Did that feel good or what! Girl, you look like you've had a complete makeover. Do you love the new you're becoming? Yes, I can see the new godly woman taking formation. You've made progress, but I need you to be patient no matter what comes your way. Just a reminder, the enemy watches when God allows improvement and every time you make progress. He will come to test your faith. Yep, he is coming for you! I need you to go deep into your cupboard and pack a huge lunch. We are getting ready for a road trip to a city called, *Trusting the Process*. Bring some extra sandwich bags. The road might get a bit bumpy and curvy, causing you to vomit, and the rental van needs to be free of upchuck.

Before you get ready for bed, please write down all the things you saw in the mirror that captured your *Godly Womanhood* and the things that did not. (note 5) Okay! Get some rest, and I'll catch up with you tomorrow.

NOTE 5

My Devotional Thoughts

Would you please write down and meditate on all the things you saw in the mirror that captured your Godly Womanhood and those that did not?

____

____

____

____

____

____

____

____

____

____

____

____

Prayer

Gracious Father, when I look in the mirror, I see all the things I am not. All the things that do not reflect the image of You. God grant me the serenity to accept the things I cannot change, the courage to change the things I can, and the wisdom to know the difference. Your words say that you are a restorer of faith. I asked that You open my eyes to see the beauty, the purpose, and the new territory you have waiting for me. I declare no weapon formed against me shall prosper. Please help me accept the Godly Woman you created and purposed me to be in Jesus' Name. Amen.

Scriptures of Meditation

"The one who gets wisdom loves life; the one who cherishes understanding will soon prosper."
(Proverbs 8:35-36, NIV)

"For those who find me find life and receive favor from the Lord. But those who fail to find me harm themselves; all who hate me love death." (Song of Solomon 4:7, NIV))

"You are altogether beautiful, my darling; there is no flaw in you." (Song of Solomon 1:15, NIV))

"Great are the works of the Lord; they are pondered by all who delight in them." (Psalm 92:4-5, NIV)

"After all, no one ever hated their own body, but they feed and care for their body, just as Christ does the church."
(Ecclesiastes 4:5, NIV)

"Those who are kind benefit themselves, but the cruel bring ruin on themselves." (2 Timothy 3:1-3, NIV)

"But now thus says the Lord, he who created you, O Jacob, he who formed you, O Israel: Fear not, for I have redeemed you; I have called you by name, you are mine."
(Isaiah 43:1)

CHAPTER SIX

TRUSTING THE PROCESS

"Faith is Trust not only in God's promises but also in God's process."

Kendra

Hello girlfriend, thank you for showing up. I'm excited about this road trip and hope we can reflect on the promises of God. Are you comfortable? Let me give you a little sequel of the journey before we get on the road. God gives a specific expectation for you as a woman and a pretty independent foundation for application to your life. You will have circumstances in your life that orchestrate your life's direction.

All you have to do is trust His process and obey His will.

Trusting God will never take you to where He doesn't want or needs you to be. Although some of your most significant victories will come after your most painful experiences, be patient and trust the process! Okay, buckle up, girlfriend. I'm excited about this journey of helping you to understand what it takes to trust God to transform you to full *Godly Womanhood.*

Trusting God will never take you to where He doesn't want or needs you to be.

The process can be complex without seeing a clear picture. It can make it hard to trust; however, you must use what you're going through as momentum. Even when you don't comprehend the process, God works it out for your good. Trust was hard for me, and I will admit that after all the violations, rejection, and abuse in my life, it was difficult to trust people; I even found it difficult to trust God.

I discovered I'd been in survival mode most of my life due to being held hostage to my past. So my guard was up; I trusted little; few could get in. Not even God because I was a bucket full of pain. But thank God for His marvelous works in me! Finally, He delivered me from the distress. Now I can trust more, build up others, and trust with a guarded heart. It was a journey in that wilderness but thank you, LORD!

If you ask me how I survived and got to where I am today, it was the rejection. It's not a good feeling, and it hurts like hell, but it's part of the process. So if you have ever been overlooked, pushed aside, or misused, I would like to congratulate you! Why am I congratulating you? Before you slam the book on this page, let me break it down a bit more with one of my wounded little girl stories?

As a child growing up in Los Angeles, there was nothing more complicated than identifying who I was. When I turned seven, it was the summer of May; I glanced in the mirror while brushing my teeth and realized something different. My skin did not resemble the rest of the family. Instead, I was a lot lighter than they were. Strangely as it seemed, I was a product of my mom and dad, a light, somewhat vanilla chocolatey color little girl. I did not like my ivory color skin. I wanted to be dark like the rest of my family. Little did I know the true essence of my ivory skin and difficulties would help me grow into the woman I am today. Yep, God was starting the process even back then. At seven, I learned the difference between physical qualities and internal strength.

There was a new story to tell each year as I grew up. Finally, it was six years later, and not only was the color of my ivory skin creating enemies, but I did not feel like I was suitable in the world. Most of the kids in my school were dark in color. It was far beyond the sixties and into the error of the seventies when racial segregation among African American children was prevalent.

There was color division in the school and some thought being light skin was better than being dark skin. The fairer skin people thought to be, the more elite. I remember one negative experience, one of my classmates picked a fight with me to prove the yellow person, as they called us, could not fight. I was eating my lunch in the cafeteria when suddenly a voice appeared out of nowhere and said, "You think you're better than the rest of us, yellow girl." Then came the push to the back of my head, and we began to rumble all over the cafeteria until the principal broke us apart. It wasn't a surprise when I got the wood paddle laid on my bottom and given a few days' suspension. This incident caused me to have self-doubt and hate myself. I wanted to fit in where ever I could, so I spent much of my life rejecting the way God made me. Thus, I would devote adolescence and a large portion of my adult life to attempting to alter what God had already created.

There was a process taking place in which God was using this situation to propel me into the next dimension of my life. But, in the meantime, He allowed me to take the wheel and wander in the wilderness for a while. Because eventually, I would have to rely on him. And after seasons in the rebellion of His process, I understood my transition was not only a destination but a decision to trust His process.

Are you suffering from the wounded "Little Girl Spirit"? Let me pull over and give you a healing affirmation:

THE LITTLE GIRL

Wounded by the pain, remembering and reminiscing,
The scars from my childhood dreams, she cries out for me,
The little girl inside screams, please help me!

Protect me from these things, these people they hurt me,
The scars have left me so empty; Lord,
help me to feel this void,
The little girl inside screams, please rescue me!
Haunted by the past, allowing false love to rule me,
Tormented and abused just to fill the vacancy,
Trusted and vulnerable to the enemy,
The little girl inside screams, please pray for me!
A fixer spirit and mentality, lens no peace,
To this broken vessel, who cried out for peace?
Ashamed and alone, my past rules me,
The little girl inside screams, I'm
drowning; please save me!
Misjudged and mistaken because of my character, history,
Tears are shed, my heart is torn, and
no one understands me,
Uniquely built through all these tragedies,
The little girl inside screams, God, do you hear me!
Never forgotten, He answered me,
You were never alone; I'd never abandon thee,
The little girl who cries out is now set free.

Roberta L. Robertson

I know it's easier said than done but let the Lord be your chauffeur driver. Learn from me; I chose to take the wheel when God did not ask for any help, as I mentioned earlier. If you decide to take your route and use your own resources instead of following His path, the road will lead to a dead end. Know that God is a reliable source by His works, but when you choose to take shortcuts and pursue your own direction. Like the Israelites who had physical sight but lacked spiritual insight (Roman 11:8). It will cause you to become lost, delayed in your journey, or held captive in your mess. So, girl, you look a bit motion sick, get that plastic bag out and hold on. I did tell you the road would be a bit bumpy.

Let's look at what you need to get into the right lane and on the right road in trusting the process from female to *Godly Womanhood.* Are you getting excited about this road trip yet? Let me change the radio channel to something more upbeat!

First, you must trust God in the process

To be elevated to a level you never occupied, you must be willing to endure a season of discomfort you've never experienced. When God allows you to go through a Moses journey, he's not punishing you but merely trying to elevate you to a new level of maturity and opportunity. Concentrate on this sentence; the will of God will never lead you into a season where His supernatural covering will not provide protection.

Faith is acting in response to God speaking, and you must be tuned in with God. You must be on the right radio channel, or you won't get the information needed to reach your destination if you listen to the wrong station.

The faith of the Israel people was being tested. God had given the Israelites confirmation through signs and wonders along the journey. He performed many miracles to confirm that He would get them to the Promised Land. God also required them to trust Him and step out of their box. He told Moses to use his staff, and the Sea path would open (Exodus 14:21, KJV). He had already said that the water would stop flowing as soon as they set foot in the Jordan River. They had the promise. They had to be willing to trust that He would do all that He had said He would do. They must have felt the temptation of unbelief. What if nothing happens, what if we don't make it through, or what if we die?

If the river stops flowing before reaching it, no faith is required. And if all the doors open and the path ahead is crystal clear, what would you need to rely on God for. Faith is acting in response to God speaking. The next step belongs to you if God has told you to do something or trust Him in a particular situation or destination. Then, God acts and fulfills what He said He would do as we take that step.

<u>Second, you must allow God to order your steps.</u>

God knows the beginning and the end, but He will not give you the complete picture of your path. Instead, God takes you through a Saul experience, allowing the scales to fall upon your eyes (Acts 9:18, NLT). If he showed you the big picture, you would die in the process. There would be no need for a test, no reason for a transition, and no impartation.

When traveling on your path to full *Godly Womanhood*, God only gives you a brief view, just enough to get you to where He wants you to be or what He desires you to see. Have you ever noticed that you can only see so far when traveling down a road or highway? You won't know what's ahead of you unless your eyes capture the attention of the posted signs. You won't know whether there is a stop sign, a roadblock, construction delays, a detour, or whether the road is straight or curved.

A female mindset will have you caught up in what's ahead, and you become blinded by what is in the present. You will zone out; you'll ignore all posted signs; the ones that say stop here and pray, dead-end on Worry Lane, Stress Blvd closed, and make a U-turn and return to the altar. You'll get ahead of God's plan, not allowing God to order your steps (Psalm 37:23). Instead of staying on the road of Damascus, you become distracted and miss your conversion. Please understand your transition connects to the process, which connects you to God's steps for your life.

You can't allow the enemy to be a back seat driver. You may not like the process; it will get a little bouncy, hit a few potholes, and run out of gas. But you have to endure the journey because God is trying to transition you to another level.

You must understand the enemy is not mad because of where you are but because of where God is trying to transition you. When you are in God's grace, you are heading towards transitioning from female to *Godly Womanhood*. It may not always feel like it. But, God's path is draped with promise, and it is through God's grace you will capture your transformation.

You must understand the enemy is not mad because of where you are but because of where God is trying to transition you.

Finally, you must decide

You will have to get out of the mindset of "decision" and move into the perspective of "I have decided." Not making a decision creates mental warfare due to uncertainty. You must decide to trust God with your life. It would help if you resolved to transition from female to *Godly Womanhood without fear*. You must also be intentional about what you decide and speak over your life to be confident that He who began a good work in you will complete it. (Philippians 1:6)

"Being confident of this, that he who began
a good work in you will carry it on to
completion until the day of Christ Jesus."
Philippians 1:6
New International Version

Do you need a restroom break? I'm going to pull over at the next rest stop, The Road to Success; please read the map of life posted on the wall when we get there.

The Road to Success

There are curves called failure,
A loop called confusion,
Speed bumps called friends,
Caution lights called family, You will have flats called jobs.
But if you have a spare called determination,
An engine called perseverance,
Insurance called faith,
A driver called Jesus,
You will make it to a place called glory

Author Sulaymon Tadsee Faozohny!

I'm so glad you made it up the hill with the tight turns and winding roads without getting motion sickness or puking. But, before we get back on the road, please write down everything you don't trust about this process to *Godly Womanhood. (note 6)*

Please copy the below affirmation, place it on your bathroom mirror, and read it daily for inspiration.

Take one day at a time.
Matthew 6:34

Remember, all things work together for the good
Romans 8:28

Under no circumstances should you worry.
Philippians 4:6

Start every day with prayer a supplication.
I Thessalonians 5:16-18

The Lord will never leave you are forsake you.
Hebrews 13:5

NOTE 6

My Devotional Thoughts

Would you please write down everything you don't trust about this process to Godly Womanhood? And Why?

____

____

____

____

____

____

____

____

____

____

____

____

Prayer

Dear Lord, help me trust in You with all your heart; and keep me from not depending on Your understanding. Help me seek Your will in all I do, and show me which path to take. I commit everything to You, Lord, and I trust You with the process from female to Godly Womanhood.

Scriptures of Meditation

"Trust in the LORD with all your heart, and do not lean on your own understanding. In all your ways acknowledge him, and he will make straight your paths." (Proverbs 3:5-6, ESV)

"Delight yourself in the LORD, and he will give you the desires of your heart. Commit your way to the LORD; trust in him, and he will act." (Psalms 37:4-5, ESV)

"Our soul waits for the LORD; he is our help and our shield. For our heart is glad in him, because we trust in his holy name. Let your steadfast love, O LORD, be upon us, even as we hope in you." (Psalms 33:20-22, ESV)

*"You keep him in perfect peace whose mind is stayed on you, because he trusts in you. Trust in the LORD forever, for the LORD GOD is an everlasting rock."
(Isaiah 26:3-4, ESV)*

"Behold, God is my salvation; I will trust, and will not be afraid; for the LORD GOD is my strength and my song, and he has become my salvation."
(Isaiah 12:2, ESV)

"And those who know your name put their trust in you, for you, O LORD, have not forsaken those who seek you."
(Psalm 9:10, ESV)

CHAPTER SEVEN

SEASONS IN THE VALLEY

"Being with God on top of the mountain is great, but knowing you built your relationship with God in the valley is awesome."

Mark Robinson

A few retreats in the valley are vital to understanding the need to rely on God for your transition from female to *Godly Womanhood.* Okay, girlfriend, the cabin is a few miles away? So please fasten your seat belts, and let's get on the road. Alright, we are here; get unpacked and settle in. The tour guide (Holy Spirit) will be waiting for us at the valley's edge.

When you are in your deepest, driest, and darkest valleys, you will experience the need to call upon Abba the Father. For example, when you are strong out on life, feeling abandoned, broken, and out of options, and the wounds are so bad, you are entirely bled out. You have no oxygen left, and you feel you can't breathe, and you feel yourself fading away.

It is during these most painful and dramatic moments that you seek God. But fortunately, you have just enough energy to muster a prayer to God for help with a snotty nose, bent over on your knees, and a spewing out stomach kind of prayer. It is what I call being in the valley of dry bones. At this point, you are at a complete thirst for God. You may even run into David in the valley from the book of Psalms 63:1 encouraging you with a prayer. "O God, thou art my God; early will I seek thee: my soul thirsteth for thee, my flesh longeth for thee in a dry and thirsty land, where no water is." So this is the time when you put yourself in a position to develop a closer relationship with God.

Often you reach the bottom of the valley, and you think God is punishing you. I assure you He is not punishing you. Instead, He's preparing you for something far more significant. It is the transition from female to *Godly Womanhood.* Don't fear! Trust Him!

There are seasons that you can become so worldly absorbed you hallucinate in the valley. God allows you to get to the point of disgruntlement in your life to pull you away from the temporary things of the earth so you can focus on the extraordinary of eternity. I know it feels good when everything appears to be going your way but remember, the things of this earth are only temporary.

A Thirsty Situation

Listen, let's get back to David for a moment. Do you know his thirst was real? He was in a thirsty situation! Most of the time, when people pray, they're in desperate situations. And a lot of the time, we thirst after all the wrong things, becoming power-thirsty. The only power we should possess is the power that comes from God.

The worldly and material thirsty things that we possess in this world cannot be taken into heavenly places:

- ❖ *Husband thirsty* - God must be first.
- ❖ *Children Thirsty* - release them to God.
- ❖ *Money Thirsty* - money is the root of all evil.
- ❖ *Physical Thirsty* - we only want to satisfy the flesh.
- ❖ *Control Thirsty* - we can't control any more than what God gives us the authority to control.
- ❖ *People Thirsty* - looking for others to quench their thirst.
- ❖ *Revenge Thirsty* - let God take care of your enemies.

"Blessed are those who hunger and thirst for righteousness."(Matthew 5:6, NIV)

When the wilderness caused David weariness, discomfort, and thirst, his flesh cried out in unison with the desire of his soul. He wasn't in the comfort of his home or the Army quarters; he was in the middle of the desert in a dry and weary place with no water, no food, and no shelter. His thirst was real! But listen, David isn't consumed with thoughts of the world or revenge thirsty. Nor was he petitioning for his position or possessions to be restored. Instead, David was thirsty for God as the deer that panteth for the water.

Let me tell you how thirsty this brother was! Listen, David took the time to write psalms while he was in a desperate, dry, and weary place. Would you take the time to write psalms in your journal while you are hungry, hopeless, and thirsty? David knew God intimately and personally and spent time with God before this dry and dehydrated situation. He became victorious over discouragement due to his prayer thirst for God.

Like David, you may find yourself in a thirsty and dry situation. So you must encourage yourself in the Lord! And not emphasize the circumstances or people for reassurance, or you will be dissatisfied every time.

Don't forfeit your promises for discouragement! I assure you God promises provision; He promises restoration and reconciliation. He promises deliverance; He promises salvation for those who will drink of His water. But you must take notes from David, kick discouragement to the curb, and desire to have a thirst for God.

When you have a prayer thirst, you begin to speak a prayer thirst language. You start to cancel every assignment that comes to destroy and prevent God's purpose over your life. You begin to speak authority over every dry situation in your life. You will not only speak the language, but you will also start to have a prayer thirst walk. You begin to walk in the power of God's authority. You start to walk in strength to cast out demons and warlocks that come up against you. You begin to declare the gates of hell shall not prevail against thee. Girl! Are you thirsty?

Chapter 2 mentions that the woman who met Jesus at the well was thirsty enough to drink His living water. To possess the power to do those things that I describe, you must decide if you're thirsty enough to drink the living water. If you don't drink the water, your relationship with God will dwindle and become depleted in your transition. You will stay in your sin, and your soul will die in the valley.

During specific seasons a valley is a cold, dark, and rainy place, and it can be a place of uncertainty. You will experience terrains, which will require you to switch up your gear. It's full of temptations and unexpected visits from the enemy. And it's not a place where you want to be for long periods. But they are necessary when God is transitioning you from female to Godly Womanhood.

<u>My Valley Experience</u>

Let me share a specific situation in my valley experience. During the peak of my teen years, I was a student-athlete walking home from a day of basketball practice. A young man decided to walk with me; he was as smooth as butter in his conversation. Music was the amplifier of my life. I loved it! He used it to persuade me he had tapes of some of my favorite artists. But, little did I know, he was a predator seeking to take full advantage of my naivety. He convinced me to take an alternative route home and into his house, where he sexually assaulted me. Bad things do happen to vulnerable people.

God had nothing to do with the violation, but He later used it as an elevation into a closer relationship with him. He used situations like this and others as part of the process of my transition into *Godly Womanhood*. Although it was not visible in the process at the time, God turned so many of my victim experiences into victorious outcomes. God will not always explain the circumstance in our life. But He plans to take you to something greater than where He brought you.

He will not always explain the circumstance in our life. But He plans to take you to something greater than where He brought you.

Recall I mentioned God doesn't give a complete view of what's ahead. But He promises never to leave us or forsake us. So God doesn't provide details of the process because we would give up on the promise. So instead, He gives us the vision of the promise and then throws us into the process. So whatever your valley experience,

God has a plan for it and will use it to make you a master builder of life.

For God to elevate you to another level, you must be tried and tested. It is your tests and trials that develop your relationship with God. I like what televangelist Robert Schuller says about afflictions. He says, "Problems are not stop signs; they are guidelines." They deter us from the enemies' traps, help us stand amid our storm, and help keep us on the right track.

But you got this, girlfriend! First, the tour guide (Holy Spirit) will lead the way and get you through. Then, on the other side of the valley, you'll run into King David again, and he will remind you, "Yea, though you walk through the valley of the shadow of death, you will fear no evil; for God is with you, His rod and His staff, they comfort you." (Psalms 23:4, KJV)

I know you are probably thinking, let me turn back and go straight to the cabin. Hang in there and stay with me. I promise you will make it to the other side of the valley to the mountain top.

You will be taken out of your comfort zone during your tests and trials. Therefore, you must be prepared to travel into the unknown, and your faith must be strong to endure because the Lord does not give us the spirit of fear. (2 Timothy 1:7, KJV)

Sometimes when our faith is weak, it may not be apparent when life is going smoothly and we are not going through difficulties. But when hard times come, a weak faith will be revealed for what it is. Listen, God doesn't test us because He doesn't know how strong we are. Instead, He tries us because we don't know how strong we are. The testing of faith can come in small ways and even daily irritations; they may also be severe afflictions and attacks from Satan. But, whatever the testing source, it is to our benefit to undergo the trials that God allows.

God doesn't test us because He doesn't know how strong we are. Instead, He tries us because we don't know how strong we are.

The valley's design is to gracefully break you and build character and endurance. It stretches you to a level of change that you would not be able to do on your own. God has a purpose for all your valleys, and it is to build testimonies that will benefit the promotion of the kingdom of God.

At times you may feel lost in the valley. Yea, I know you are questioning why the tour guide did not provide maps. Well, girlfriend, you won't need a map in this valley! But you must follow God's plan and directions. When you are going somewhere you have never been, maps can be helpful. But no map, no matter how detailed, will tell us where exactly we need to go. Remember, God has our destiny at hand. No one else can travel to your destiny or through your valley.

Think of it this way; if you purchase a city map, it will show you how to maneuver through many parts of the town. You expect the map to tell you how to get anywhere in the city. But remember, the places you are trying to go are off the beaten path where no one else has ever gone. A map does not tell you what roadblocks are ahead, what obstacles will be in your way, what giants you will face, what devils you will encounter, or what tools you should pack to reach your destination. Only God carries the detailed map and supplies you need for your destiny. He will bring you to and through the dry land. When the Israelites were released from captivity, God sent them on a detour, not on the shortest path but through the course that would require His purpose to be fulfilled.

If you say, "God, I trust you, and I submit and surrender my path to you," something extraordinary will start to happen in your life because God will use you to do His will and His purpose. God will take you out of the mindset of a female and into an attitude of *Godly Womanhood*. If along your journey:

You say: "It's impossible."
God will say: All things are possible
(Luke 18:27)

You say: "I'm too tired."
God will say: I will give you rest
(Mat.11:28-30)

You say: "I can't go on."
God says: My grace is sufficient
(II Corinthians 12:9 & Psalm 91:15)

You say: "I can't figure things out."
God says: I will direct your steps
(Proverbs 3:5-6)

You say: "I can't do it."
God says: You can do all things
(Philippians 4:13)

You say: "I'm not able."
God says: I am able
(II Corinthians 9:8)

You say: "It's not worth it."
God says: It will be worth it
(Roman 8:2)

You say: "I can't manage."
God says: I will supply all your needs
(Philippians 4:19)

You say: "I'm afraid."
God says: I have not given you a spirit of fear
(II Timothy 1:7)

You say: "I don't have enough faith."
God says: I've given everyone a measure of faith
(Romans 12:3)

You say: "I feel all alone."
God says: I will never leave you or forsake you
(Hebrews 13:5)

The Holy Spirit is your tour guide in the valley, and He has laid the foundation to get you to the other side of your valley. Are you ready for your valley experience?

Okay, get your valley jumpsuit, helmet, and sword, and let's go!

Avoid disconnections with God

There is often no connection with people, things, or even essential resources in the valley. These things seem valuable but not as helpful as your connection with God. There might be some areas in the valley where you might experience poor connection. Losing contact with God in the valley is like a dropped call on your cell phone. Girl, you know how frustrating that can be! First, you lose temporary communication. Then you can't hear the other person on the other end. They keep talking, but you can't hear them. Sometimes there can be several reasons for the dropped call.

You can have lousy service in a bad service area or need to switch services to avoid loss of temporary connection with God. So how do you prevent a poor relationship with God?

- ❖ First, you must read and understand your contract with God and stay in His word. His word is your contract, and it helps keep you connected to God amid all your valleys, afflictions, temptations, and the midst of your trials and tribulations.
- ❖ Number two is that you must avoid the wrong service area and stay out of areas that cause poor communication with God. While you are in the

valley, you will run into Satan, but don't get into a conversation with him. And don't let him dictate your conversation with God.

❖ The third one is to know when to replace your phone. If you're not hearing God on the other end and have constant disruption, you should consider switching services. For example, you might consider a service that causes fewer dropped calls while in the valley. Then, you can talk to God no matter where you're at, which will give you unlimited access. In other words, stay away from things and people, places, and things keeping you from communicating with God.

Girlfriend, let's huddle up for a moment! Listen up when you're halfway through the valley. First, your past will call you; it calls you none stop. Then you'll get a call from the twin name depression and anxiety. But it won't stop there; you will continue to get calls from cousins like discouragement and defeat, who will merge the call with criticism and judgment. But I advise you not to pick up the phone! These calls can be a distraction to cause you to lose focus on the transition.

Next, you will experience people who are still bound by their sin and operating in the stubborn patterns of their flesh. They become a bad influence and drag you into parts of the valley where you lose focus of your progress. And when you do, I will need you to reflect on the mirror and remember how far you have come.

Just a quick nugget remember that God is only a phone call away in your darkest valley. And when He calls you, answer the phone!

The Holy Spirit provided you with some tools, and one of them was a sword(word of God). Pull it out and use it to declare you are victorious and break yokes and strongholds over your life. If you swing it towards Psalms 34:18, many are the affliction of the righteous. God says there is going to be affliction in our lives. According to the King James dictionary; afflicted means to be pressured. The further we stay away from God, the more complex the pressure becomes. So keep swinging even in your afflictions.

I love the biblical account of Job, who is afflicted when God allowed Satan to test the reality of his faithfulness by over-whelming him with disease and misfortunes, but when the pressing was over, God allowed the oil to flow. So even though Job was pressed on every side, God did not allow him to be crushed. And he stayed connected to God. So keep swinging your sword, girlfriend!

You heard it! You read it! The valleys are needed to help you get back on track and help you transition from female to *Godly Womanhood*. Some circumstances will try to draw us away from God. Things that will test our faith; worry, fear, anxiety, hate, rage, greed, lust, racism, injustice, poverty, sickness, and disease, but all these things are going to pass away. God is our refuge and strength, an ever-present help in trouble. "Therefore we will not fear, though the earth give way and the mountains fall into the heart of the sea, though its waters roar and foam and the mountains quake with their surging." (Psalm 46:1-3, NIV)

The sun is going down, and it's too late to keep going, so let's pitch a tent tonight. So we spent some time understanding why it's essential to sustain a steady connection with God. So get some rest, and we'll talk about keeping our eyes focused on heavenly things and why it's critical to the transition in the morning.

Keep your eyes focused on heavenly things

Good morning, Girlfriend! Let's jump right into this dialogue. When God molds us for His purpose and work here on earth, criticism will come from every direction. Sometimes we don't understand what God is doing with us, and it will cause us to be perplexed. What is perplexed? It means to be at a loss. It's hard when we go through a situation that we don't understand, and it causes us to fill the void with worldly stuff and people.

If we do a self-check, we can often see the level of perplexity. If we look in our closets, check our refrigerators, check what we are watching on TV, check what we're reading, check out what we're wearing, and check the conversation we are having and the people in our circle. Then, we'll know if we are focused on heavenly things. So it's a true saying you will know what is essential in your life by examining where you spend most of your time.

Often we become so emotionally involved in what is before us we don't see what is coming behind us. Then we find ourselves in parts of the valley where we are most vulnerable. Therefore, we cannot worship the things of this world, keep our eyes on heavenly things, and expect not to get lost in the valley.

Let me take a few moments to talk about that brother I mentioned in an earlier chapter who experienced a few perplexities while in the valley. Once a Christian slayer and was converted to a follower of Jesus Christ, Paul experienced much criticism (2 Corinthians). The Jews criticized his preaching, authority, and power; they said he was weak. Nevertheless, he was sometimes at a loss and did know what to do. Although he was perplexed, he was not despairing and was committed to keeping his eyes on heavenly things.

You will have haters, dream blockers, and naysayers in your valley, but no weapon formed against you that will prevail (Isaiah 54:17, NIV). So shake all the noise around you and follow the water stream toward the sun where the Holy Spirit leads you to the mountain.

There is a sense of joy in knowing when we are perplexed in our valleys, but we focus on heavenly things. Simplicity kicks in, life on earth becomes more straightforward, and our worldly needs fewer. We began to have a heart of David. We begin to activate the fruits of the spirit, putting on the whole armor of God, clothed with the power of the Holy Spirit, and girded in righteousness. However, after keeping our eyes on heavenly things, we must understand that God is our backbone.

Let us take a rest over the next hill. Catch your breath and please grab a cup of coffee, I'm going in deeper, and I want you to be fully awake.

There is absolutely no way to transform from female to *Godly Womanhood* without persecution. It comes with the assignments in our lives. We can't avoid it, we can't run from it, we can't minimize it, we can't fast forward it, and we can't even skip it, we can't dismiss it, and we certainly can't go around it. But God always equips us for the battle. Hint as to why we have valley experiences. Each valley we go through it prepares us for the next one.

You have to realize what God has put inside of you. You must remember that nothing can happen without God's permission, and God will not allow a difficulty unless He has a design purpose.

The more God begins to use us; the more skeptical folks will become. But catch this nugget! God may be using the skeptics to bend us, shape us, and make us more useable. We have to stop looking for man's approval. We don't need it to approve what God is doing in us. There is joy in knowing that in Psalms 16:9, a man's heart plans his way, but the LORD directs his steps.

Listen, TD Jakes puts it this way he says " People will hate you, environments will deny you, communities will limit you, and mentalities will poison you." But God will have your back.

In another season, a valley can be bright and sunny. It can bloom beautiful flowers and show the manifestation of God's creations. No matter how dark and dreary one season can be in the valley. If you do the work, you can always depend on God to guide you into a blossoming season of transformation. It doesn't matter what dysfunction you were in; if you keep walking through the valley, you'll walk right into His grace; you can look back at those skeptics and say thank you, and keep moving.

It won't matter who talked about you or what criticism you endure; if you keep on walking through the valley, you'll walk right into His blessings. Just stomp on the devil's head and say thank you but no thank you and keep moving toward the mountain. It isn't about who was skeptical or didn't believe in you; if you keep walking, God will release joy in your situation that can not be unraveled.

Look ahead! Girlfriend, can you see the peak of the mountain from here? Of course, in my Jimmy Cliff voice," You can see clearly now that the rain is gone." Are you ready to climb that mountain? Let's go!

Before you begin the climb to the mountain top, start building your basket of expectations. First, write your perplexities from your journeys in the valley. Then, complete your prayer to invoke God's presence in your life. (Note 7)

NOTE 7

My Devotional Thoughts

First, write your perplexities from your journeys in the valley. Then, complete a prayer to invoke God's presence into your life.

____

____

____

____

____

____

____

____

____

____

____

____

Prayer

Heavenly, Father though I walk through the valley of the shadow of death, please teach me how to trust in you and have faith in my valley. Thank You, Father, that You are the Living Water. I come to You thirsty and dehydrated. I am thirsty for your presence, and I long to be content with You. Thank You for the water that flows from every rock, stream, and desert and for allowing your Living Water to soak in the dry place of my valley. Please help me pull down every stronghold that would cause dryness in my spirit. Today, I declare that every dry area will be restored and filled with a cup running over, my dry heart will be refreshed, and I will be transformed from female to Godly Womanhood. My tongue will be lubricated with your word. I release a prayer thirst over my life. And I ask these things in the Mighty Name of Jesus.

Scriptures of Meditation

"Have I not commanded you? Be strong and courageous! Do not tremble or be dismayed, for the Lord your God is with you wherever you go." (Joshua 1:9, NASB)

"Fear not, for I am with you; be not dismayed, for I am your God; I will strengthen you, I will help you, I will uphold you with my righteous right hand."
(Isaiah 41:10, ESV)

"For such is God, Our God forever and ever; He will guide us until death." (Psalms 48:14, NASB)

"The Lord is with me; I will not be afraid. What can mere mortals do to me? The Lord is with me; he is my helper. I look in triumph on my enemies." (Psalms 118:6-7, NIV)

"By this, we know that we abide in Him and He in us, because He has given us of His Spirit." (1 John 4:13, NASB)

"Behold, God is my helper; The Lord is the sustainer of my soul." (Psalms 54:4, NASB)

CHAPTER EIGHT

BATTLE WITH SATAN ON THE MOUNTAIN

"God is up to something, or the devil wouldn't be fighting you this hard. You're going to win!

Spiritual Inspiration

The celebration begins when you cross the valley after fighting many giants and slaying some goliaths. You were tried by fire, thirsty in the valley, and partook in the forbidden fruit. But it isn't over yet, girlfriend! Recall I said in a previous chapter that we will be fighting this fight until the day we die. So get out your hiking sticks or poles, boots, crampons, rock climbing shoes, helmets, and climbing harness. If you plan to make it to the top of the mountain, stay planted in the transition from female to *Godly Womanhood*. The gear will be essential to keep the devil out of your head, house, business, and life.

The devil is a gangbanger, and when he rolls up on your mountain, your household on your job, in your marriage, in your church to do his drive-by, he comes deep with his homies. He will do everything possible to shift God's transitioning in you and keep you from reaching the top of the mountain. He comes with his homie's rejection, separation, restriction, frustration, and destruction.

The devil is a straight Christian buster, and he wants to devour you, destroy you and kill you. But if you don't see him and his boys or girls coming, you will get wiped out. So, you'll need a supernatural authority and power to get him away from your mountain.

Let me keep it real with you, girlfriend. Suppose you are not prepared and are blindsided! Then, you're going to get your butt kicked spiritually and snatched right off the side of your mountain. Then, you will be in "The Rumble in The Jungle" fight of your life. You'll come out of the ring looking and feeling like George Forman, who fell for the rope-a-dope against Muhamad Ali.

As you keep climbing up the mountain toward victory, the devil will start by sending his rejection homie. He will approach you when you least expect it. He's the subtle kind and will play games with your emotions. As you watch others around you being elevated to their mountaintop, he whispers in your ear. You will never make it! Or you can't do it!

The *Rejection Homie,* this one comes to attack your mind. He wants to make you feel like you're not wanted, not worthy of the transition from female to *Godly Womanhood, and* you're not a part of God's kingdom. He wants to cause mental warfare. Let's pause and bring Paul back into the picture for a moment. After his conversion to Christian discipleship, his community would no longer accept him. They rejected him as a Roman citizen because he stood for the principles of God (The book of Acts). And like Paul, as you are fighting in your transition, you may even experience some friendly fire and often feel rejected and run into opposition. Your adversaries will appear in many forms, including church family, friends, and even your children or spouse. And before you know it, Mr. Rejection will cause you to go into isolation. You can fall back down the mountain, feeling like you've made no progress.

You'll find yourself back in the valley and moved out of the will of God. John Ekhart says you cannot be double-minded in your test. "A double-minded man is unstable in all his ways" (James 1:8, KJV). So it would help if you keep looking in the mirror, remind yourself of who you belong to, and declare your steps continued to be ordered by God.

It is essential to understand that someone else's mountain is not your mountain. Sometimes God will keep you hanging on the side of the hill to protect or hide you from something. So, don't let the devil convince you you need to climb faster than the pace God is ordering you to do.

Okay, you survived the first round and headed into the second round. But remember all the intercessors, spiritual mothers, and fathers who are helping guide you through your transition. The devil will try to convince you they're not in it for your good. He will attempt to make you think your husband, children, boss, and even your pastor are against you and is setting you up. If you fall for that trap, you'll separate yourself from your support group. And bam! Just like that, he's got you right where he wants you. Lonely, depressed, and suicidal.

You will keep looking back down the hill wanting to go backward. You will have a strong urge to connect yourself back with folks of your past. They'll be at the bottom of the mountain, throwing hooks to pull you down. There is one thing I do know when dealing with this homie, do not consider yourself yet to have taken hold of it. But one thing you do: Forget what is behind and strain toward what is ahead. (Philippians 3:13, NIV)

The *Separation Homie,* this one comes to try and separate you from God. Satan will attempt to destroy you through other people. He uses people to steal your wealth and joy from you to try and ruin your reputation and detour you from the promises of God. God has the treasure waiting for you at the end of your valley experience, and He wants you to get to the mountain top. There will be folks who will try to hinder you from your transition, snatch your treasure, block you, talk about you, blackmail you, and tell you that there is no treasure; those people are called treasure blockers. God wants to seal your destiny. Your wealth is in the journey, test, and trial. So, you better kick the devil in the head and tell the devil to step back. The Lord has already given you the power to conquer your journey and pass the test.

There will be folks who will try to hinder you from your transition, snatch your treasure, block you, talk about you, blackmail you, and tell you that there is no treasure; those people are called treasure blockers.

Your halfway up the mountain. I'm going to need you to dig deep into the hill. So, pull out your mountain boots and your climbing harness. It's going to get a little rocky in this round. The devil will throw in his frustration, homie, so be careful. The wind is going to come hard at you. Nothing will stop the current of this dude, but if you grab hold of your sword and stake it deep into the ground of your spirit, mind, and heart. No matter how bad the wind blows, you will not be moved. Nothing will disrupt your peace, not the naysayers or your past as you climb. Keep your eyes on the mark of the high calling. (Philippians 3:14)

In this next round, the *Frustration Homie,* this one wants to frustrate you right out of your promise and your transitional climb to *Godly Womanhood.* He intends to stagnate you and cause you to stumble. He'll keep pressing you and poking you in your weakest area and nudge you until you crawl back into your box. Paul was tested when a demon-posed slave girl followed him around for four days torturing him(Acts 16:16-18). But we must be like Paul, recognize what it is, and have the power to cast it out, call it for what it is and stand for Christ.

No matter how hard the devil comes at you, keep pushing and punching your way through and declare you are victorious. A half punch will not do. I will need you to throw a combination punch and a few uppercuts. You have to keep pulling your way to the top, and God's hand will pull you up the rest of the way. So, don't give up, don't give in, and keep stretching and pressing your way. God wants us to lay aside every hindrance and the sin which so easily ensnares us. So, run with endurance the race that is set before you. (Hebrews 12:1, ESV)

You have gained some momentum, but the devil is relentless. He thought he could knock you out with the last homie. But, instead of him wiping you out with his frustration, homie, he throws in his restriction homie. Girlfriend, you got this! Don't let him corner you to the ropes! Bring your valley fighting spirit, and let's toss the devil off his game.

The *Restriction Homie,* this one will attempt to restrict your authority and power. Satan will try to lock you down so that you don't have access to God's authority. The devil will snatch your keys, but you better use your David's bone, knock the devil in his head, and take back your keys. He wants to limit you. And make you believe you can't make the transition into a godly woman, that you cant bind mental warfare, be delivered from your junk, or be lifted out of your brokenness.

Pull your sword out of your side belt and chop off the devil's head. Then use your mouth as a weapon against him and speak the word of God. Speak loudly and declare the Lord has given me the keys of the kingdom of heaven; whatever you bind on earth will be bound in heaven, and whatever you loose on earth will be loosed in heaven (Mathew 16:19, NIV). God gives us authority and dominion over every mountain in our life.

I want you to take back all the strength the devil has taken from you. Exhale, now put your back into it! Lean into it! Loose peace in your mind, joy in your spirit, transformation, increased territory and endurance over your life, and loose and command every restriction over your life to decrease by the power and authority of Jesus Christ.

Now I want you to bind every evil spirit against you and your mind, everything keeping you from transitioning to *Godly Womanhood*. Declare fruitfulness in your life, bind and cast out all enemies and declare and increase boundaries in Jesus' Name, Amen.

The devil is agitated and has tried you with almost everything he's got. But, he knows what God has in store for you on the top of the mountain. You will be tenacious in your gift and calling, unstoppable, renewed your strength when you get there. You will have a new walk, talk, and be clothed with righteousness.

You are in the final round, and the devil will come at you with an extra lean. So take your position and don't hold anything back. He is getting ready to throw everything he's got into the ring. The destruction, homie, is coming for you. So put your big girl draws on, and let's do this! What does destruction mean? Well, I'm glad you're curious to know! It means tearing down or dismantling and destroying the core from the inside out. So make no mistake about the closer you get to your mountain top, the stronger the enemy will come for you.

**The closer you get to your mountain top, the
stronger the enemy will come for you**

The *Destruction Homie, this* one will attempt to destroy you and your family. I know I have made this analogy a few times. However, I must keep reminding you that the devil only comes to kill, steal, and destroy (John 10:10, ESV). You can't be a punk in your test or trial. It will help if you run to your cross, not away from it. Listen, when you operate with the power and authority of God, can't anybody deter you? Can nobody take you out, not even the devil. So stand your ground, don't flinch, and do not fear those who kill the body but are unable to kill the soul; rather, fear Him who can destroy both soul and body in hell. (Matthew 10:28, NASB)

When God allows Satan to test us, He makes us aware of who He created us to be. Powerful, more than conquers, highly favored, inheritors of the kingdom so that we can be sure of ourselves in Him. So, we are prepared for the attacks of the devil and his homies. God tests us to make sure we are qualified to be trusted with the gifts, purpose, and talents placed inside of us. So, we stay connected to His principles, remain humble, and not seek world approval but His approval. So that our testimonies are free of error, mixed motives, or hidden agendas, when we make it to the mountain top, we are prepared for the next one.

The views from the mountain top are grand, unlike any picture you have ever seen. Please take it all in and listen to God's voice. God is raising a remnant out of the crevices and the darkness. He is raising up godly women to be His mouthpiece and demonstrate His power and glory. You will continue to be tested and go through changes and experience shake-ups, but through it all, you will have to remain hungry, seeking what God has to say in His Word. Whether you are obedient, standing, kneeling, or laid out on the floor in prayer! If you face attacks from every side of the enemy, you are part of that remnant.

There is one thing I know for sure God is positioning you for destiny because He is about to have His grandest display of glory on the earth, and you are it! He has chosen you! And your transition to *Godly Womanhood* will become part of the testimony He will use so that others might see His glory, faithfulness, sovereignty, and grace in your life.

It has been a hell of a journey climbing to the mountaintop, and it took prayer, faith, endurance, and drive to get there. Please write down some of the things that kept you from falling from the side of the mountain. And some of your strengths and weaknesses to reflect on will help you when you reach your next peak. (note 8)

I pray you brought a life jacket because you will be released to ride the *Rivers of Life* in the next chapter.

NOTE 8

My Devotional Thoughts

Please write down some of the things that kept you from falling from the side of the mountain. And some of your strengths and weaknesses to reflect on when you reach your next peak.

____

____

____

____

____

____

____

____

____

____

____

Prayer

Dear Abba, there is no other God like You. You know every battle I will come up against. You see, every mountain I will face. Lord, bless my weaknesses and my strength. Lord, let me be blessed in my struggles and blessed in my victories. Lord, let me be blessed to be above and not beneath. Lord, let me be blessed to be the head and not the tail. Lord, let me be blessed with dominion and victory over the enemy. Lord, let everything my hand touches be blessed. Lord, let your blessing overtake my life." In Jesus' Mighty Name, Amen

Scriptures of Meditation

"The righteous cry, and the LORD hears and delivers them out of all their troubles." Just a reminder that God is all we need to overcome spiritual attacks.
(Psalms 34:17, NASB)

"Through You, we will push back our adversaries, through Your name we will trample down those who rise up against us." (Psalms 44:5, NASB)

"Submit yourselves to God. Resist the devil, and he will flee from you." (James 4:7, NSAB)

"Behold, I have given you authority to tread on serpents and scorpions, and over all the power of the enemy and nothing shall hurt you." (Luke 10:19, NASB)

"Do not fear them, for the Lord your God is the one fighting for you." (Deuteronomy 3:22, NASB)

"The Lord will cause your enemies who rise against you to be defeated before you. They shall come out against you one way and flee before you seven ways." (Deuteronomy 28:7, NASB)

"No, in all these things we are more than conquerors through him who loved us." (Romans 8:37, ESV)

"Put on the full armor of God so that you can take your stand against the devil's schemes. For our struggle is not against flesh and blood, but against the rulers, against the authorities, against the powers of this dark world, and against the spiritual forces of evil in the heavenly realms. Therefore, put on the full armor of God so that when the day of evil comes, you may be able to stand your ground, and after you have done everything, to stand. Stand firm then, with the belt of truth buckled around your waist, with the breastplate of righteousness in place, and with your feet fitted with the readiness that comes from the gospel of peace. In addition to all this, take up the shield of faith, with which you can extinguish all the flaming arrows of the evil one. Take the helmet of salvation and the sword of the Spirit, which is the word of God." These verses carry all the answers. (Ephesians 6:11–17, NIV)

CHAPTER NINE

THE CONVERSION

*"Being a Christian is more than just instantaneous
conversion – it is a daily process whereby you
grow to be more and more like Christ."*

Billy Graham

All right, girlfriend, as you head down the backside of the mountain into the *Rivers of Life*. Know that no matter how high or rough the current of the waves in your life, you have been given spiritual tools for the sail, and the Lord has prepared you as you walk in your transition and transformation to *Godly Womanhood.* He wants me to pass these words on to you, "He that believeth on me, as the scripture hath said, out of his belly shall flow rivers of living water."(John 7:38, KJV)

125

Straight out of the box! You have stepped out of the female spirit into a *Godly Womanhood* spirit. You've awakened to a new standard of living, responsibility, sacredness, love, and authority. But, it will require you to live your life with consistent prayer, discipline, repentance, and faith.

Check your gear for a spiritual life jacket; you may need it from time to time to help you stay afloat while sailing along the river. Your spiritual life jacket is Jesus, so when you feel like the river's current is too strong, call His name, and He will calm the waters.

There will be seasons on your sail when pollution and sewage will surface from the bottom of the river, and it will cause an entanglement around you. Sometimes the web of trash can cause such disruption in your sail you will need to step out of the boat and walk on water toward Jesus to be rescued.

I'm reminded of the account in the bible in Mathew 14 when Peter's faith is tested. A windstorm arose as they were at sea sailing across the Sea of Galilee. The wind causes the ship to be tossed with the waves. They called for Jesus, who was on a different boat, and He walked across the water toward them. Although skeptical. Peter challenged Jesus by saying, Lord bid me come to you if it's you. So Peter left the boat and walked on water toward Jesus. But when the wind started to pick up, he lost his focus on the Lord and began to sink.

There will always be constant disruption in your life that will try to take your focus off the Lord, even more so in your conversion from female to *Godly Womanhood*.

Becoming a godly woman is not a quick fix to all life's problems. Girlfriend, you thought your battle on the mountain with Satan was a struggle. In the *Rivers of Life*, you will encounter the same demons but different spirits. Don't trip! You are equipped!

The *Rivers of Life* can be overwhelming, and you will often feel like you are drowning. But when you choose to walk into this transition, it comes with the good, the bad, and the ugly. When you are following Jesus, it is not easy and comes with much ridicule and persecution. But, remember, you are not sailing for a day or just a month; you are sailing on the *Rivers of Life* for eternity.

***You are not sailing for a day or just a month;
you are sailing on the Rivers of Life for eternity.***

Now that you have committed yourself and work unto God, everything you do should align with His principles. Everything you harvest should reflect what you have learned if you are in His word. There should be more actions of a woman than female actions, which should reflect an abundance of fruit. Applying this model can assure that your life's plans match up with God's plan. You will begin to do what I call the divine shuffle with God!

You may find yourself sailing along in life; it appears everything is all good, and then suddenly you find yourself not moving on the river; you may feel like there is no movement, and God has abandoned you.

But, I promise you He has not and is there with you. And will provide you with a breath of momentum in your stillness. God does some of his best work on the river and specializes in the impossible! Just like He calmed the waters for Peter, He will create waves of movement to push out all the sorrow, suffering, temptation, and test you encounter keeping you from mobility. God will always be your guide on your journey home.

A Journey Home

Don't be concerned about a thing,
for don't you know it's true
A devoted Father has launched the
ship that gently carries you!
Each boat that sails about the rivers of
life that rock with every storm,
Is guided through the channels of faith,
To a harbor safe and warm.
The hand that binds you in the womb
Will never cease to care balance in the wildest wind,
A love that's always near to the very end.
And each woman hears a special call
that summons her alone,
While God provides along the way
The light that guides her home
To the golden throne of grace.

Roberta L. Robertson

But as you grow stronger in His word, your journey in the *Rivers of Life* should start to exude some fruits of the spirit, love, joy, peace, patience, kindness, goodness, faithfulness, and self-control. (Galatians 5:22, NIV)

On the other hand, there may be seasons when you are sailing way too fast. It causes you to miss opportunities for God to stretch or grow you. So, occasionally He will slow the pace of the sail to get your attention. It will feel like it lasts for days, months, and even years. But, the storm will only last to the level of your disobedience. And long enough to rid the distractions and draw your attention back to Him.

Girlfriend, one of the most amazing things about our Father, is he is no slick Ricky; He will never stand you up and always makes Himself available. And Isaiah 43:2 is here to remind you that Jesus is with you on your sail. He will be with you when you pass through the waters, and they shall not overflow you through the rivers. The tour guide did not forsake you in the valley, climbing to the mountain top, and He surely won't abandon you in the *Rivers of Life*.

When I look back on how far the Lord has brought me, I remember seasons of drowning in the *Rivers of Life*. There was a time when my head was entirely underwater. Yet, He allowed me to sink just enough to remind me His spirit was dwelling within me. So I could fight my way back to the surface. I love the quote, "A boat doesn't sink because of the water around it; it sinks because the water gets into it. Don't let what's happening around you weigh you down." *Author unknown*

Just like the ship, we can allow the things of the world to cause us to sink in our conversion to *Godly Womanhood.* It starts with a surface of water getting into the boat, and then as the currents become more intense, the water begins to emerge into the entire ship. And before you pump the water out, the boat has sunk. Similar to the analogy, we are the vessels sailing for Jesus Christ. And one of His requirements to keep the boat sailing is to pump out the water before it sinks. If we allow water to enter our boat or become so corrupt by jobs, money, worldly expectations, society, or people around us, we are useless to the Kingdom of God. We will be in no position to pick up the stranded and lost along the journey.

God's ultimate plan in transitioning you from female to *Godly Womanhood* is to sail you down the river into the sea so you can catch more fish. So you start in the murky waters of life, operating in a female spirit, not knowing God has a plan to turn the dark water into rivers of living water and purpose. And through His conversion of you and His infinite grace, He took every one of your single life experiences to draw you near to Him, redeem you, and bring you to a level of spiritual strength so you would walk in your purpose and assigned appointment on earth.

God legitimately owns every part of you and everything in your life. Therefore, He has every right to expect the best from you. His word says, return to me, and I will return to you." (Malachi 3:7, NLT) No matter how far you sail away from Him, He is always there to reroute you and get you back on course. So, before we get to the end of the channel where the river waters will merge into the sea, let me share how to avoid a leaky conversion.

No matter how far you sail away from Him, He is always there to reroute you and get you back on course.

Listen, girlfriend, you will be evolving throughout this new journey. So let me be very upfront with you there will be seasons when your river will entirely run dry. Life will continue to take you through some difficult times. You may feel you are in a place of perpetual dryness and desperation, and it will feel like a Jordon River experience.

But let me encourage you to pull out that spiritual life jacket. There is no river too dry, vast, or too fast that He can't fill, divide, or close; when you have the presence of the Lord, there is nothing impossible. If you believe everything, His word says you should expect every adversity to be overcome with victory. But you will have to be careful of the possible leaks. Leaks turn into flooding, and flooding turns into you sinking.

<u>Avoiding a leaky Conversion</u>

Drifting in the *Rivers of Life* means we have completely lost focus and lack the discipline to His word or pulled away from God. So what am I saying to you? Well! Girlfriend, you fell off the wagon. You have returned to the female attitude and ditched your *Godly Womanhood.* Yep, it can happen!

Let me slap this hook on your boat! You may have to purchase a small spiritual pocket mirror to carry in your nice Coach purse as a constant reminder of where He transitioned you. Every once in a while, you will need to pull it out and examine yourself to see whether you are in the faith. Test yourself. Or do you not realize this about yourselves, that Jesus Christ is in you? Unless, indeed, you fail to meet the test. (2 Corinthians 13:5 ESV)

This scripture shows us that drifting comes through a lack of discipline. We don't ordinarily deliberately plan to go astray, but whether we do or not, the result is the same regardless of the intention. There is a consequence. The closer we are to the word of God, the further we are from sin, and the less likely we are to become leaky in our conversion. The further we are from God's word, the closer we are to sin, and the more likely we will become leaky in our conversion.

The closer we are to the word of God, the further we are from sin, and the less likely we are to become leaky in our conversion.

The further we are from God's word, the closer we are to sin, and the more likely we will become leaky in our conversion.

"People do not drift toward Holiness. Apart from grace-driven effort, people do not gravitate toward godliness, prayer, obedience to scripture, faith, and delight in the Lord. We drift toward compromise and call it tolerance; we drift toward disobedience and call it freedom; we drift toward superstition and call it faith. We cherish the indiscipline of lost self-control and call it relaxation; we slouch toward prayerlessness and delude ourselves into thinking we have escaped legalism; we slide toward godlessness and convince ourselves we have been liberated." *D.A Carson*

To avoid drifting from His presence, find yourself an accountability partner who will hold you accountable to prayer and obedience. If you don't, I'll be waiting for you back in chapter one. It's all good! It happens to the best of us. Sometimes we're on the right road, just headed in the wrong direction, and may need to return to the alter.

Don't Allow yourself to get distracted on your journey if you don't see immediate abundance in your life. It's okay to question God's direction. But remember to keep traveling on your own path. Igorness can cause you to move ahead of God's plans, and it may cause you to want to get in somebody else's lane. Girlfriend, ignore Mary Jane on the left and don't speed up to try and pass Barbie Sue on your right. Yes, it looks good from your passenger side window, but we don't know the road God allowed them to travel. God wants you to stay in your own lane. Stay focused! He'll tell you when to switch lanes and change direction.

We are about ten minutes out from the docking area. So, let's meet on the top deck, and let me share with you my written testimony.

My Conversion from Female to Godly Womanhood

Personal testimonies are supposed to be three to five minutes. I suspect this written version of my conversion from female to Godly Womanhood violates that rule. Now, if you were to press me to identify one verse that I would associate with my salvation or walk with Christ, it would be "Brethren, I do not regard myself as having laid hold of it yet; but one thing I do: forgetting what lies behind and reaching forward to what lies ahead, I press on toward the goal for the prize of the upward call of God in Christ Jesus" (Philippians 3:13-1, NASB)

There were times when I found it challenging to make sense of the experiences I had in my life before and even after I met Jesus Christ. I was conflicted and had several questions about my life. Why did I grow up in such a bad home environment? Why was I raped? Why did my husband beat me? Why can't I ever get ahead? Why was I abused? Why are my children so defiant? I can go on and on about the whys and how comes, but I'm sure you may have a long list of your own.

At a very young age, I discovered a vast world out there, and there were some very awful things happening. As I edged through my adolescent years, I went from being a fretful child to a teenager often plagued by severe anxiety and phobias: I feared domestic violence, relationships with people, and the world. I prayed little during these years, and although I had received the Lord in my life at age 13, I was uninspired by it and rarely thought of God or had no interest in anything spiritual. My spiritual sleep was all but awakened, and the darkness of my anxiety also began to manifest as intense anger. As a result, my spiritual life and, if any, my relationship with the Lord went into deep remission.

Unfortunately, I will not be able to entirely articulate every step. Still, in varying stages of my teenage and young adult life, God began to place spiritual people in my life strategically. It began a continuous stream of impartation in my life that started a yarning in me for purpose.

One day, I took a complete view of my life's history, the roads I had traveled, and the storms, struggles, or tragedies in lamens terms. I thought to myself there has to be some significance to these events. But, if so, are they relevant to my life's purpose, and would they positively impact others?

I reference these experiences to storms of faith. Getting through those storms took courage, faith in God, and determination. When I didn't maintain a close relationship with God, I often entered a storm with a no-hope attitude, blame, and confusion. I was not always clear about what I should do to get through the storm and what I needed to stand amid the storm. I've asked myself how I made it through so many of those storms.

I found that God gave me favor, and His grace sustained me through every one of my storms. There were times when I caused my own storms by not seeking God or His word. However, there were also storms that I had no control over. As a result, I often got angry, and I was quick to blame God and everyone else for my circumstances.

My character and mind were challenged through the storms, and my spirit was often broken. It revealed all of my fears, doubts, and weaknesses. But I didn't realize that those same storms prepared me and strengthened me for storms to come. The process helped me build a stronger character, conquer fear and renew my spirit.

These storms were my testimonies to those in similar circumstances. As I deepened my relationship and walked with God, I realized that the inner spirit determines my external strength. Thus I am no longer drinking the milk but enduring the meat of God's word; I have continued to feed my spirit some substance, knowledge, and impartation. Going through the storms had two possible outcomes; either building character and eternal life or creating a lost soul. Often, knowledge and wisdom come with time, and the more I trust in God, the less I worry about the outcome.

When I look at the deep valleys I went through; I realize that God was there even when I didn't seek Him and when I was lost. He was calling for my attention. Yes, the Lord penetrated my heart and gave me a new mind and spirit as I built a stronger relationship with Him. I knew Him through His Word and the effects of His sacraments in my life. I knew by faith He existed, but I had not fully surrendered.

I needed deliverance and healing over those areas in my life that hindered my entire relationship with the Lord and the purpose He had for my life. I cannot describe my healing experience to you or His glory, for it is beyond words. There were no words necessary; it was like the heart speaking to the core. Yes, I had fully let Him in again.

Over the years, my experience of Him in prayer has deepened; it has also become gentler. Some days His presence is more profound than others, and other days, I struggle to see Him at all. But quite faithfully throughout the last several years, I have known His presence.

Jesus came and saved my soul; He also saved my life in this world, for I am here alive all these years later despite my storms. I recall Mary, who rejoiced at the mighty work of God in her life; so do I rejoice; "My soul magnifies the Lord, and my spirit rejoices in God my savior....For the Mighty One has done great things for me holy is His name." (Luke 1:46, 47,49, ESV)

I want to close out this chapter by encouraging you with these words, "You have the power to change the course of your life's direction, your family, your community, and the world." Jesus Christ bridged the gap between God and us in His death on the cross; therefore, this is where you will find all of your life's answers. Never underestimate God's ability to change the course of your life, no matter how bad it may seem.

The boat is preparing to dock at the shore of the city, and you will be released; And before you set foot in the town, I declare and speak life over you in the below prayer:

Prayer of Thanksgiving

Today, Father, I want to thank You for the blessing of transformation and restoration over this godly woman. Thank You for softening her heart so that she will make good decisions with a clear mind.

I declare that You are smiling down on her and that your favor will be in everything she does.

I decree that she will be blessed in the city and given favor in her discovery, blessed going in and blessed going out.

In this prayer, I speak Psalm 84:11 that you are blessing her with favor and honor, and no good thing from her because her walk is blameless. Grant her now Father the spirit of obedience that exudes strength. In Jesus' Name, Amen.

NOTE 9

My Devotional Thoughts

Write down everything causing you to drift on Your River of Life. But, then, I want you to toss it in the river and not even think about jumping in to retrieve it.

____

____

____

____

____

____

____

____

____

____

____

____

Prayer

Almighty and gracious Father, thank You for providing me with a place of refuge. Thank You for allowing me to dwell in Your secret place and abide under Your shadow. Thank You, Lord, for being my refuge and fortress and giving me strength in every season of my life, my God; I will trust You. Therefore, as I walk in my conversion, I declare You shall deliver me from the fowler's snare and the noisome pestilence. And Lord, I ask that You cover me with Your feathers, and under Your wings so that I may declare your trust: and I decree Your truth shall be my shield and buckler. In Jesus' Mighty Name, Amen

Scriptures of Meditation

"I can do all things through Christ who strengthens me."(Philippians 4:13, N, NKJV)

"The Lord is my strength and my shield. I trust him with all my heart. He helps me, and my heart is filled with joy. I burst out in songs of thanksgiving." (Psalms 28:7, NLT)

"In the day when I cried out, You answered me and made me bold with strength in my soul." (Psalms 138:3, NKJV)

"O God, You are more awesome than Your holy places. The God of Israel is He who gives strength and power to His people." (Psalms 68:35, NKJV)

"He gives power to the weak, and to those who have no might He increases strength." (Isaiah 40:29, KJV))

"For the Lord will be your confidence, and will keep your foot from being caught." (Proverbs 3:26, NKJV)

"Yet the righteous will hold to his way, and he who has clean hands will be stronger and stronger." (Job 17:9, NKJV)

"They shall walk after the Lord. He will roar like a lion. When He roars, then His sons shall come trembling from the west." (Hosea 11:10, NKJV)

"If you faint in the day of adversity, your strength is small." (Proverbs 24:10, NKJV)

CHAPTER TEN

THE DISCOVERY

*"The Kingdom Woman is not Perfect.
She is a Transforming Woman."*

Tony Evans

Congratulations! You have arrived at the city of discovery. Your purpose and identity will be evident as you walk through the city streets. You have resilience and stamina. No one will recognize you as your strut will be different; you will have a new swag and language. You will walk in authority and confidence, and your steps will be directed to a purposed ground. You know who you are and whose you are. But don't get a "Big Head," stay humble and walk out the manifestation of your transition of *Godly Womanhood.* Understand that no woman has it fully together; remember, we were all filthy and dirty females God saved by His grace. He invested in us when we chose not to invest in ourselves.

Girlfriend, it has been a pleasure, but this is where my journey with you ends. It's time for you to go flow in your calling! First, however, I want to leave a few more nuggets before you step into your new season and territory.

Let me remind you to remain one with Him. You can no longer count on your own righteousness through obeying the law; rather, you become righteous through faith in Christ. For God's way of making you right with Him depends on faith (Philippians 3:9-10, NLT). His word is full of truth, and it is the strategy you will need to walk in the full manifestation of your discovery consistently.

Yes, girlfriend, you have reached the discovery point of who you are in Christ Jesus. I am very proud of you! But let me remind you to always believe who He says you are. And expect all adversities in your life to end with a victorious outcome. Just remember, self-doubt comes through looking at your own merits. And it will cause you to question God's favor in your life.

Nevertheless, you are righteous and worthy of being blessed and prosperous in His eyes. So He has crowned the godly woman in you with glory and honor. And guess what, girlfriend, it did not cost you a dime. God earned it for you!

Even though Jesus earned it for you, It still requires you to walk through the city in faith to see the revelation of His favor in your life. Then, your dedication, commitment, and obedience in your transition will begin to unleash your gifts and assignments and a pre-scheduled divine appointment with your destiny. There is an ease in knowing that nothing can alter that appointment, whatever circumstances you face.

You've conquered the valley, climbed and battled Satan on the mountain, and tossed in the rivers. Now you must be willing to flow and operate with God's anointing as you take on this new territory. You will have to live out God's expectations through His divine power and authority. You will need the mental strength, courage, and boldness to lean into it. And without it, there will be no manifestation of His power.

There must be spiritual confidence for your spiritual gifts to be unleashed. With this confidence, there is no anxiety, fear, or worry. But I can't let you go just yet; you'll need just one more thing to help you develop courageous trust.

Spiritual Gifts Unleashed

Before entering the city, the Holy Spirit wanted me to let you know about a disclaimer! When you begin to unleash your spiritual assets, everyone will not be happy about your spiritual gifts or purpose. Your gifts aren't always going to offer splendor; they can provoke kayos, making you wonder if it is a gift from God or a plot from the enemy. Yes, I said that! I did!

Whatever our spiritual gifts are, God will be revealed. So your kingly gift was not for the asking; it was for you to step into spiritual maturity with the whole will of God over your life.

You will discover many gifts that you did not realize you had; it isn't until you begin to exercise those gifts that you will see the manifestation of them. You must allow the Holy Spirit to dwell within you and the release of fear and people to be moved for those gifts to develop and grow. The minute your gifts manifest, the naysayers will come out of the basements and try to disrupt you from using your talents, mainly the devil. It's all good! I want you to thank every hater and naysayer you come across. They are helping you get that much closer to your destiny. There will be gift snatchers all over your assigned territory, and their assignment is to stop you from activating your frozen assets/gift through fear and intimidation.

Listen, I think you know by now not to take the enemy for granted. But, girlfriend, by no means is the devil done with you yet. You will be under constant spiritual attack, and you must be aware of your surroundings and ready for the enemy. Anything significant that the Lord has in store for you the enemy wants to destroy.

I'm jumping up and down because something about when the enemy comes after a strong godly woman gets me excited! You know you are powerful when he walks through the city recruiting you to a fight. It will cost the enemy something every time he messes with you. So when you walk into that new job, open up that business, get that promotion, start that ministry, give birth to your dreams, start walking in your divine calling, shut them down and let them know to keep you out of their mouth.

Your spiritual conception and vision have been planted but not yet birthed. The word of God tells us to "Write the vision and make it plain on tablets, that he may run who reads it. For the vision is yet for an appointed time, but at the end, it will speak, and it will not lie. Though it tarries, wait for it; because it will surely come, it will not tarry" (Habakkuk 2:2-3, KJV). You must continue to spend intimate time with God, studying His word, seeking spiritual mentoring, and developing your spiritual gifts. So that God can continue to impart wisdom and anointing, you need to fulfill your life's purpose.

On the other hand, there is an old saying, if the devil ain't messing with you, something is wrong. So if you are not on the devil's most wanted list, you'd better do a self-check. Maybe you are leaning back into the female ways, not in the word of God, or you've been intrigued by a new box you are trying to squeeze back inside of.

Girlfriend, don't go into your city or territory and become the walking dead. Instead, use everything God has planted inside you and given to you through this process to evoke the trajectory of your God-given vision. He will finance the vision and support it. But, first, you have to trust it! Create it! Walk-in it! Then watch Him build it! You ready!

And remember that when you walk through the city, walk by faith and not by sight (2 Corinthians 5:7, ESV). God will not lead you anywhere where He does not send His security guards grace and mercy. Sing this affirmation as you walk down the town's streets; many blessings to you!

Serving with Faith

Whatever the job
No matter the race,
Through all the storms
We must seek His face,
It's not for accolades that we work in faith
But to be an example of His glorious grace,
For in our good works
It's not men that we aim to please
But God, who is worthy of all victory,
We must press with diligence
without pride or gluttony,
Working from the heart with grace and diplomacy,
For God gives no reward for status or titles
But promises eternal life
through our commitment and honor,
So you see if we give God complete control
we are never denied access
through the kingdom doors,
We must strive for obedience
to acknowledge God's authority,
Seek His name
for it is the strong tower

no evil can conquer it,
Through all adversity
it provides safety from the enemy,
Building a union with God
Will grant you access to His almighty power,
Serving in faith, God will reveal to you His will, His grace.

Roberta L. Robertson

NOTE 10

My Devotional Thoughts

What has God revealed about your purpose, vision, and assignment? Write down what He has spoken or shown to you.

____

____

____

____

____

____

____

____

____

____

____

____

Prayer

Heavenly Father, thank You, for there is no weapon formed against me that shall prosper. Thank You for Your promises, and I believe You will do everything in me that you said You would do. I trust You have kept me hidden until now, a time such as this, for Your glory. Please open my eyes to see Your marvelous work in me. Open my ears to hear your voice, and keep my heart pure and humble. And I praise Your son Jesus for His process on the cross so that I have this opportunity to reach a point of revelation. I ask that You walk and be with me on this evolving journey into the godly woman you created me to be. In Jesus' Name, Amen

Scriptural Meditation

"For I know the plans I have for you, declares the Lord, plans for welfare and not for evil, to give you a future and a hope." (Jeremiah 29:11, ESV)

"For still the vision awaits its appointed time; it hastens to the end—it will not lie. If it seems slow, wait for it; it will surely come; it will not delay." (Habakkuk 2:3, ESV)

"The Lord will fulfill his purpose for me; your steadfast love, O Lord, endures forever. Do not forsake the work of your hands." (Psalm 138:8)

"I have said these things to you, that in me you may have peace. In the world you will have tribulation. But take heart; I have overcome the world." (John 16:33)

"So shall my word be that goes out from my mouth; it shall not return to me empty, but it shall accomplish that which I purpose, and shall succeed in the thing for which I sent it." (Isaiah 55:11, ESV)

"Commit your work to the Lord, and your plans will be established." (Proverbs 16:3, ESV)

And we know that for those who love God, all things work together for good, for those who are called according to his purpose. (Romans 8:28, ESV)

"For I know the plans I have for you, declares the Lord, plans for welfare and not for evil, to give you a future and a hope. Then you will call upon me and come and pray to me, and I will hear you. You will seek me and find me when you seek me with all your heart. I will be found by you, declares the Lord, and I will restore your fortunes and gather you from all the nations and all the places where I have driven you, declares the Lord, and I will bring you back to the place from which I sent you into exile." (Jeremiah 29:11-14, ESV)

AFTERWORD

When I started writing this book, I was not immediately obedient to the Lord whispering in my ear. I would hear His voice in the late-night hours and early in the morning. He said, your obedience will make room for you and prosper you! The voice of the Holy Spirit would speak to me consistently to the point I could not ignore it. I would say to the Lord, I'm not a writer, and I don't think this is one of the gifts you blessed me with.

The Lord begins to speak to me and let me know He has downloaded in me everything I need to complete this book, and He is ready to activate it. But unfortunately, it took me more than two years to complete this manuscript through some resistance, mental warfare, and sickness.

When I finally put time aside to begin writing the first chapter, I initially did not realize God was using every page to transition me out of my disobedience. However, once I got to the 4th chapter, I was exposed, and I had been drifting away from His presence. The purpose He so clearly created me for had been placed on a shelf collecting dust.

God needed to remind me why He transitioned me from a female to *Godly Womanhood.* God gave me the vision in the transition, but it would never come to fruition until I vowed to be obedient to it. He was doing a new thing in me right amidst this book, and girlfriend, I pray these words met you at an appropriate time and place in your life.

God has a desire to demonstrate to you a splendid vision for your life. And it is not about where you are but the direction He is taking you. But, as long as you have breath in your lungs, the enemy will do everything to keep you from the foreknowledge of your vision. The same way God spoke to me, He will talk to you and give you insight into your dreams and visions. But, the closer you are to your vision, the more the enemy tries to kill and destroy it.

When we are born into this world as a female, exposure to environments, people, and experiences help to shape the very elements of our core. However, it is not until we meet Jesus and build a relationship with Him that we begin to transition into the best versions of ourselves.

A female is limited when it comes to hearing the voice of God, and it is evident He has to wash us clean and transform us to *Godly Womanhood* to reach a purposeful life. It doesn't mean we will be perfect. It simply means we will get rid of the worldly female life and step into a life of abundance and favor. The transformation allows us to hear His voice and build a relationship with God that brings revelation to our divine purpose and destiny. Jesus came that we may have life and have it more abundantly. (John 10:10b, KJV)

I'm so thankful you chose to take this journey. I see you like a caterpillar coming out of your cacoon, becoming a beautiful butterfly; it will become more evident as you heal and step into your purpose and assignment.

I hope you will share this book with a female needing revelation, transformation, and deliverance. God says there are so many more hidden treasures that He wants to expose, and He has identified every female from the womb. He wants to kill everything they have attached themselves to for identification.

Thank you so much for taking steps to walk through this process. Girlfriend, I love you dearly and will hold you close to my heart and in my prayers as you walk in your transition from female into Godly Womanhood. God bless you!

ACKNOWLEDGMENTS

Writing this book was the most gratifying thing I have ever done and, by far, very intimidating. It required a lot of things but foremost, being in a suitable space spiritually and mentally. However, it was impossible without support from family, friends, and intercessory prayer.

First, I want to acknowledge my Lord and Savior, Jesus Christ, for extending His grace upon me. He is my best friend, my comforter, and He loved me even when I did not love myself. I am so thankful for the manifestation of the vision; He spoke to me. I worked a full-time job as a Director and oversaw over 500 employees while writing this book. And He made the impossible possible, and I am so grateful that I walked in His obedience.

To Pastor Glen Robertson, my husband and life partner in everything I do. Babe, I did it! It is complete, and I'm so thankful for your prayers and encouragement. Thank you for your unconditional love, patients, and understanding as I journeyed through this process. You are my Boaz, and I am thankful to God that He allowed us to share the same space and time.

Thank you, Pastor Michael J. Henderson, for your intercessory prayers and guidance. You took the time to read through the drafted manuscript and wrote the forward to this book, and it is so appreciated. Thank you for your inspiration, for keeping me focused on the big picture, and providing constructive feedback. God bless you and First Lady Kenyatta Henerson.

To Pastor Anthony and Bishop Jackie Green, you were the consistent spiritual father and mother who grounded me in biblical principles of faith, prayer, and deliverance. Thank you for the unconditional love and intercessory prayers. Without a spiritual foundation, a house can not sustain life's storms. Bless you for your discipleship and teachings through the years.

Finally, a special thank you to every female God has placed in my path and allowed me to share my testimony, mentor, and grow from our encounter. You are part of the reason God has created and entrusted me to walk in my purpose. I pray He blesses each of you beyond measure.

NOTES

Chapter One-The Process

1   Kingsley Glass
    https://www.yourquote.in/kingsley-glass-diaj/quotes/everything-god-
    allows-come-our-way-always-purpose-uses-even-msdho
2   Collins Online Dictionary
    https://www.collinsdictionary.com/us/dictionary/english/process
3   King James Dictionary
    https://av1611.com/kjbp/kjv-dictionary/process.html

Chapter Two-Female Versus Women

1   Proverbs 31:10, NIV
2   Nasdaq Board of DIversity
    https://www.google.com/search?q=Nasdaq+Board+Diversity+
    definition+of+female&client=firefox-b-1-d&sxsrf=APq-WBv7mnWM_
    9aoPRADbQiw5w9tM00knQ%3A1649530382214&ei=DtZRYoTf
    DP2rqtsPoOqm2A8&ved=0ahUKEwiEnunD04f3AhX9lWoFHSC1CfsQ4
    dUDCA0&oq=Nasdaq+Board+Diversity+definition+of+female&gs
    _lcp=Cgdnd3Mtd2l6EAw6BwgjELADECc6BwgAEEcQsAM6BwgjE
    LACECc6BQgAEKIESgQIQRgASgQIRhgAUJQQWIYlYJJDaAFwAXgA
    gAFiiAG8CJIBAjE1mAEAoAEByAEJwAEB&sclient=gws-wiz
3   Merriam Webster Dictionary
    https://www.merriam-webster.com/dictionary/female
4   Serita Jakes
    https://www.google.com/url?sa=i&url=https%3A%2F%2Ftwitter.com
    %2Ffirstladyjakes%2Fstatus%2F509718359944884226&psig=
    AOvVaw042zrJpkOWBem9_u20n0L7&ust=16496186480062000&
    source=images&cd=vfe&ved=0CAsQjhxqFwoTCOjL173ah
    cCFQAAAAAdAAAAABAD

5   King James Version Dictionary
     https://av1611.com/kjbp/kjv-dictionary/woman.html
6   Wikipedia -Women in the Bible
     https://en.wikipedia.org/wiki/Women_in_the_Bible
7   Marvin Sapp
     https://www.google.com/search?client=firefox-b-1-d&q=marvin+sapp
     +IHe+sees+the+bestin+you+

Chapter Three-Godly Womanhood

1   Psalms 46:5, NKJV
2   Wikipedia -Steve Harvey
     https://en.wikipedia.org/wiki/Act_Like_a_Lady,_Think_Like_a_Man

Chapter Four-Created for a Purpose

1   Faithward.org
     https://www.faithward.org/purposeful-living/
2   Rick Warren
     https://quotefancy.com/quote/899922/Rick-Warren-God-has-a-
     purpose-behind-every-problem-He-uses-circumstances-to-develop-our

Chapter Five-Acceptance

1   Adrian Rogers
     https://www.goodreads.com/quotes/1543215-grace-is-god-s-
     acceptance-of-us-faith-is-our-acceptance
2   Patty Lebelle -The best is yet to come
     https://www.youtube.com/watch?v=dI89rLaxP_4
3   Albert Einstein
     https://quoteinvestigator.com/2017/03/23/same/

Chapter Six-Trusting the Process

1   Kendra
     https://kendradueck.wordpress.com/2016/10/21/trusting-gods-
     process/

2   Victory Quote
     <u>https://me.me/i/some-of-your-greatest-victories-will-come-after-</u>
     <u>your-most-4b115225499c4126a0535ccfa2f148ef</u>
3   Sulaymon Tadese Faozahny -Road to success
     <u>https://www.poemhunter.com/poem/the-road-to-success-is-not-</u>
     <u>straight/</u>
4   Roberta L. Robertson - The Little Girl

Chapter Seven-Seasons in the Valley

1   Mark Robinson
     <u>https://www.pinterest.com/pin/403142604141809509/</u>
2   Robert Schuller
     <u>https://www.whatshouldireadnext.com/quotes/robert-h-schuller-</u>
     <u>problems-are-not-stop-signs</u>
3   T.D Jakes, The Potter's House, March 21, 2021
     <u>https://www.youtube.com/watch?v=FmNv5K50ex8</u>
4   Jimmy Cliff
     <u>https://www.google.com/search?client=firefox-b-1-d&q=I+can+see+cl</u>
     <u>early+now+that+the+rain+is+gone</u>

Chapter Eight-Battle with Satan on the Mountain

1   Spiritual Inspiration
     <u>https://www.google.com/search?q=spiritual+inspiration+quote</u>
     <u>+God+is+up+to+something+or+the+devil+wouldn%27t+be+figh</u>
     <u>ting+you+this+hard&client=firefox-b-1-d&sxsrf=ALiCzsbuDfD1</u>
     <u>CY6xzRQXJW3NQehwnrL3SA:1651446939869&tbm=isch&sourc</u>
     <u>e=iu&ictx=1&vet=1&fir=zjwiJZLlTTMyzM%252Ck8cN6jmJgV8n-</u>
     <u>M%252C_%253Btqib0L-okwoA2M%252CElXWOAmJEY7daM%</u>
     <u>252C_%253BalIXGzIrPeBxUM%252C_Mgtua_MjF3z4M%252C</u>
     <u>%253BhuZxF9OoruaLvM%252CI3twGxRzF2xRfM%252C</u>
     <u>%253BOtNYTAM6QssibM%252CZKdBqHwwsNfo6M%252C</u>
     <u>%253BLN_Cif6gUNNBJM%252C2-ksSaS4wNiSwM%252C</u>
     <u>%253B7xxdDoblT3F6hM%252CWEqO73uQqDQEAM%252C</u>
     <u>%253BsecQLcS3hyrjVM%252CpO158Q409cEn6M%252C</u>
     <u>%253BFyTSqaIih8zhYM%252Cu2r1ImVl8RPbPM%252C</u>
     <u>%253BQd7HPqcxMqQSdM%252Cm8tHPEUs6KNweM%252C</u>
     <u>&usg=AI4_-kQ-_kG3nqtGtXqwMfPXjm3veOmwDg&sa=</u>

X&ved=2ahUKEwi2jt2ht7_3AhUHrmoFHWKgChAQ9QF6BAgeEAE#im
grc=tqib0L-okwoA2M

2   John Ekhart
https://iamaruby.com/forum/topics/apostle-john-eckhart-
deliverance-from-double-mindedness-becoming-

Chapter Nine-The Conversions

1   D.A Carson
https://www.goodreads.com/quotes/99185-people-do-not-drift-
toward-holiness-apart-from-grace-driven-effort
2   Ship quote
https://leilagrandemange.com/2020/08/23/sunday-inspiration-
uplifting-quote-bible-verse-and-prayer/
3   Roberta L. Robertson - A Journey Home

Chapter Ten-The Discovery

1   Tony Evans
https://m.facebook.com/drtonyevans/photos/the-kingdom-woman-
is-not-a-perfect-woman-she-is-a-transforming-woman/643368809
009556/
2   Roberta L. Robertson - Serving in Faith